GRAMMAR
Form and Function

1B

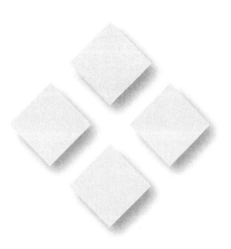

Milada Broukal

McGraw-Hill

Grammar Form and Function 1B

Published by McGraw-Hill ESL/ELT, a business unit of The McGraw-Hill Companies, Inc., 1221 Avenue of the Americas, New York, NY 10020. Copyright © 2004 by The McGraw-Hill Companies, Inc. All rights reserved. No part of this publication may be reproduced or distributed in any form or by any means, or stored in a database or retrieval system, without the prior written consent of The McGraw-Hill Companies, Inc., including, but not limited to, in any network or other electronic storage or transmission, or broadcast for distance learning.

ISBN: 0-07-301196-7

Editorial director: Tina B. Carver
Senior managing editor: Erik Gundersen
Developmental editors: Arley Gray, Annie Sullivan
Editorial assistants: David Averbach, Kasey Williamson
Production managers: Alfonso Reyes, Juanita Thompson
Cover design: AcentoVisual
Interior design: AcentoVisual
Art: Alejando Benassini, Eldon Doty

Photo credits:
All photos are courtesy of Getty Images Royalty-Free Collection with the exception of the following:
Page 146 © Stephen Studd/Getty Images; **Page 150** Mona Lisa, c.1503-6/The Bridgeman Art Library/Getty Images.

McGraw-Hill

The **McGraw-Hill** Companies

Contents

UNIT 12 SPECIAL EXPRESSIONS

UNIT 13 ADJECTIVES AND ADVERBS

APPENDICES

Acknowledgements

The publisher and author would like to thank the following individuals who reviewed *Grammar Form and Function* during the development of the series and whose comments and suggestions were invaluable in creating this project.

- Tony Albert, *Jewish Vocational Services, San Francisco, CA*
- Leslie A. Biaggi, *Miami–Dade Community College, Miami, FL*
- Gerry Boyd, *Northern Virginia Community College, VA*
- Marcia M. Captan, *Miami–Dade Community College, Miami, FL*
- Yongjae Paul Choe, *Dongguk University, Seoul, Korea*
- Sally Gearhart, *Santa Rosa Junior College, Santa Rosa, CA*
- Mary Gross, *Miramar College, San Diego, CA*
- Martin Guerin, *Miami–Dade Community College, Miami, FL*
- Patty Heiser, *University of Washington, Seattle, WA*
- Susan Kasten, *University of North Texas, Denton, TX*
- Sarah Kegley, *Georgia State University, Atlanta, GA*
- Kelly Kennedy-Isern, *Miami–Dade Community College, Miami, FL*
- Grace Low, *Germantown, TN*
- Irene Maksymjuk, *Boston University, Boston, MA*
- Christina Michaud, *Bunker Hill Community College, Boston, MA*
- Cristi Mitchell, *Miami–Dade Community College-Kendall Campus, Miami, FL*
- Carol Piñeiro, *Boston University, Boston, MA*
- Michelle Remaud, *Roxbury Community College, Boston, MA*
- Diana Renn, *Wentworth Institute of Technology, Boston, MA*
- Alice Savage, *North Harris College, Houston, TX*
- Karen Stanley, *Central Piedmont Community College, Charlotte, NC*
- Roberta Steinberg, *Mt. Ida College, Newton, MA*

The author would like to thank everyone at McGraw-Hill who participated in this project's development, especially Arley Gray, Erik Gundersen, Annie Sullivan, Jennifer Monaghan, David Averbach, Kasey Williamson, and Tina Carver.

Welcome to Grammar Form and Function!

In **Grammar Form and Function 1**, high-interest photos bring beginning grammar to life, providing visual contexts for learning and retaining new structures and vocabulary.

Welcome to **Grammar Form and Function**. This visual tour will provide you with an overview of a unit from Book 1.

❖ *Form* presentations teach grammar structures through complete charts and memorable photos that facilitate students' recall of grammar structures.

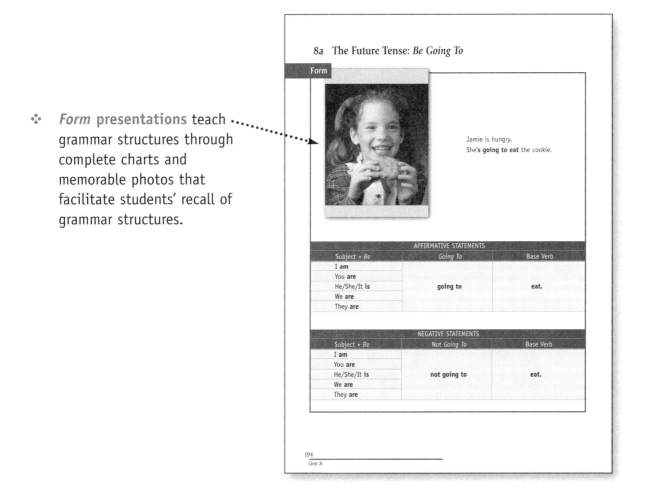

8a   The Future Tense: *Be Going To*

Form

Jamie is hungry.
She**'s going to eat** the cookie.

AFFIRMATIVE STATEMENTS

Subject + *Be*	*Going To*	Base Verb
I **am**		
You **are**		
He/She/It **is**	**going to**	**eat.**
We **are**		
They **are**		

NEGATIVE STATEMENTS

Subject + *Be*	Not *Going To*	Base Verb
I **am**		
You **are**		
He/She/It **is**	**not going to**	**eat.**
We **are**		
They **are**		

194
Unit 8

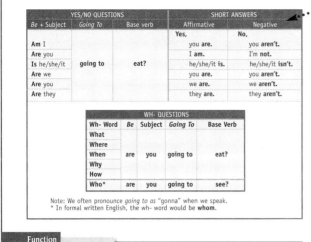

YES/NO QUESTIONS			SHORT ANSWERS	
Be + Subject	Going To	Base verb	Affirmative	Negative
			Yes,	No,
Am I			you **are.**	you **aren't.**
Are you			I **am.**	I'm **not.**
Is he/she/it	going to	eat?	he/she/it **is.**	he/she/it **isn't.**
Are we			you **are.**	you **aren't.**
Are you			we **are.**	we **aren't.**
Are they			they **are.**	they **aren't.**

WH- QUESTIONS				
Wh- Word	Be	Subject	Going To	Base Verb
What				
Where				
When	are	you	going to	eat?
Why				
How				
Who*	are	you	going to	see?

Note: We often pronounce *going to* as "gonna" when we speak.
* In formal written English, the wh- word would be **whom**.

❖ *Form* presentations also include related grammatical points such as negatives, yes/no questions, wh– questions, and short answers.

Function

Look at those clouds!
It's **going to rain** soon.

1. We use *be + going to* + base verb to make predictions about the future. (What we see is going to happen very soon.)

2. We use *be + going to* + base verb to talk about our plans for the future.

We're **going to buy** a house next year.

195
The Future Tense

❖ *Function* explanations and examples clarify when to use grammar structures.

| Practice

Look at the photos. Then complete the sentences with *be going to* and a verb from the list.

buy some fruit
drink a cup of coffee
eat an ice cream cone

hit the ball
order a meal
paint the wall

pay the bill
take a photo
write a check

1. Jim has a camera.
Jim is going to take a photo   .

2. Brad has a paintbrush.
_____.

3. Sue is in the supermarket.
_____.

4. Tony is in a café.
_____.

5. Mel has a checkbook and a pen.
_____.

6. Ted is in a restaurant.
_____.

196
Unit 8

❖ **Extensive practice** guides students from accurate production to fluent use of the grammar.

❖ **High-interest photos** contextualize the grammar and provide visual cues in practice exercises.

First page panel

11 Practice

Make predictions for the year 2050. Say what you think. Use *will* or *won't* in the blanks.

1. People ____*will*____ drive electric cars.
2. Everybody _____ have a computer at home.
3. People _____ carry money.
4. People _____ take vacations on the moon.
5. All people _____ speak the same language.
6. All people around the world _____ use the same currency (money).
7. People _____ find life on other planets.
8. People _____ get serious diseases like cancer.
9. Trains _____ travel very fast.
10. People _____ live to be 130 years old.
11. Men and women _____ continue to marry.
12. Children _____ go to school five days a week.

Discuss with your partner or the class.
Write three sentences with *will* or *won't* about what you think will happen.

12 Practice

Complete the conversation with forms of the present progressive, *will,* and *be going to.*

Julia: I (go) ____*am going*____ to the supermarket right now. Do you want anything?
                  1

Leyla: Yes. Can you get some orange juice?

Julia: Sure. It's on my list, so I (get) _____ it.
                         2

Leyla: I also wanted to pick up my photos today, but I don't have time to do it.

Julia: Don't worry. I (pick) _____ them up for you. I
                         3

          (be) _____ back soon. (be) _____ you _____ here?
               4   5   6

Leyla: I (go) _____ to work now.
                  7

Julia: OK. I (see) _____ you later. Remember Tony and Suzy
                    8

          (come) _____ tonight.
                9

207
The Future Tense

❖ Topical exercises provide opportunities for students to use grammar naturally.

Second page panel

9 Practice

Complete the dialogue. Use the present progressive of the verbs in parentheses.

Mike: What (do) __*are*__ you ____*doing*____ this weekend?
                  1   2

Jackie: Well, I'm really very busy. Tonight I (go) _____ out to dinner with
                                        3

          my friend Lulu. She's great fun. We always have a good time. Then on Saturday

          morning I (take) _____ a computer class.
                     4

Mike: Finally! You're learning to use a computer!

Jackie: Yes, I love it. I'm doing well, too. Then, after that, I (meet) _____
                                              5

          my mother. We (go) _____ shopping to get my father a birthday gift.
                         6

          Then, in the evening, I (have)_____ dinner with Chris. On Sunday,
                               7

          Chris and I (go) _____ to a friend's wedding. So on Sunday morning,
                       8

          I (get) _____ dressed, and he (pick) _____ me up to
                9   10

          go there. He (drive) _____ there. It's a long drive. We
                        11

          (stay) _____ there for the dinner reception then we
                12

          (come) _____ back at around six. Chris (fly) _____
                13   14

          to Boston in the evening, and I (go) _____ over to Magda's place
                                       15

          to study English. You know we (have) _____ a test on Monday.
                                     16

          So anyway, Mike, what (do) _____ you _____?
                      17   18

Mike: Oh, nothing really.

Jackie: My bus is here. See you Monday! Bye!

10 Your Turn

Work with a partner. Ask and answer the questions.

Example:
You: Where are you going after class?
Your partner: I'm going home.

Today	Tomorrow	On the weekend
where/go/after class	what/do/tomorrow	where/go/Saturday
how/get/there	where/go/evening	what/do/Sunday
what/do/this evening		

204
Unit 8

❖ Your Turn activities guide students to practice grammar in personally meaningful conversations.

WRITING: Describe Future Plans

Write a paragraph about future plans.

Step 1. Work with a partner. A friend is coming to your town/city for three days. It is his/her first visit. Make a list of four good places to go.

1. _____   3. _____

2. _____   4. _____

Step 2. Plan your three days. Where are you going to go first, second, third, and last? Your friend is arriving at 4:00 at the airport near your town. Ask your partner questions like these. Write the answers to the questions.

1. Are you going to meet your friend at the airport?
2. Where are you going to take him/her after that?
3. What are you going to do that evening? Why?
4. What are you going to do on Saturday?
5. What are you going to do if the weather is bad?
6. What will you do on Sunday?
7. How will you get there?
8. What special food will you give your friend to eat?

❖ **Writing assignments** build composition skills, such as narrating and describing, through real-life, step-by-step tasks.

SELF-TEST

A   Choose the best answer, A, B, C, or D, to complete the sentence. Mark your answer by darkening the oval with the same letter.

1. When I go to London, I _____ Buckingham Palace.

   A. am visiting   Ⓐ Ⓑ Ⓒ Ⓓ
   B. going visit
   C. am going to visit
   D. will visiting

2. What _____ on the weekend?

   A. are you going to do
   B. are you going   Ⓐ Ⓑ Ⓒ Ⓓ
   C. you are going to do
   D. you doing

6. In twenty years, most people _____ electric cars.

   A. are driving   Ⓐ Ⓑ Ⓒ Ⓓ
   B. will drive
   C. going drive
   D. is going to drive

7. I will be worried before I _____ to the interview.

   A. will go   Ⓐ Ⓑ Ⓒ Ⓓ
   B. go
   C. am going

❖ **Self-Tests** at the end of each unit allow students to evaluate their mastery of the grammar while providing informal practice of standardized test taking.

B   Find the underlined word or phrase, A, B, C, or D, that is incorrect. Mark your answer by darkening the oval with the same letter.

1. <u>How</u> <u>will</u> <u>be jobs</u> different in <u>the</u> future?
   A   B   C   D

   Ⓐ Ⓑ Ⓒ Ⓓ

6. In the future, <u>men</u> and <u>women</u> <u>will be</u>
                   A   B   C

   <u>continue</u> to marry.
   D

   Ⓐ Ⓑ Ⓒ Ⓓ

2. In the United States, you <u>leave</u> a tip
                              A

   when <u>you</u> <u>having</u> dinner <u>in a restaurant</u>.
        B   C   D

   Ⓐ Ⓑ Ⓒ Ⓓ

7. If sharks <u>do not</u> <u>move</u> all the time, <u>they</u>
              A   B   C

   <u>will be</u> die.
   D

   Ⓐ Ⓑ Ⓒ Ⓓ

To the Teacher

Grammar Form and Function is a three-level series designed to ensure students' success in learning grammar. The series features interesting photos to help students accurately recall grammar points, meaningful contexts, and a clear, easy-to-understand format that integrates practice of the rules of essential English grammar (form) with information about when to apply them and what they mean (function).

Features

❖ **Flexible approach to grammar instruction** integrates study of new structures (form) with information on how to use them and what they mean (function).

❖ **High-interest photos** contextualize new grammar and vocabulary.

❖ **Comprehensive grammar coverage** targets all important structures.

❖ **Extensive practice** ensures accurate production and fluent use of grammar.

❖ **Your Turn activities** guide students to practice grammar in personally meaningful conversations.

❖ **Writing assignments** build composition skills like narrating and describing through step-by-step tasks.

❖ **Self-Tests and Unit Quizzes** offer multiple assessment tools for student and teacher use, in print and Web formats.

❖ **Companion Website activities** develop real-world listening skills.

Components

❖ **Student Book** has 14 units with abundant practice in both form and function of each grammar structure. Each unit also features communicative *Your Turn* activities, a step-by-step *Writing* assignment, and a *Self-Test*.

❖ **Teacher's Manual** provides the following:
  ◆ Teaching tips and techniques
  ◆ Overview of each unit
  ◆ Answer keys for the Student Book and Workbook
  ◆ Expansion activities
  ◆ Culture, usage, and vocabulary notes
  ◆ Answers to frequently asked questions about the grammar structures
  ◆ Unit quizzes in a standardized test format and answer keys for each quiz.

❖ **Workbook** features additional exercises for each grammar structure, plus an extra student Self-Test at the end of each unit.

❖ **Website** provides further practice, as well as expansion opportunities for students.

Overview of the Series

Pedagogical Approach

What is *form*?

Form is the structure of a grammar point and what it looks like. Practice of the form builds students' accuracy and helps them recognize the grammar point in authentic situations, so they are better prepared to understand what they are reading or what other people are saying.

What is *function*?

Function is when and how we use a grammar point. Practice of the function builds students' fluency and helps them apply the grammar point in their real lives.

Why does **Grammar Form and Function** incorporate both form and function into its approach to teaching grammar?

Mastery of grammar relies on students knowing the rules of English (form) and correctly understanding how to apply them (function). Providing abundant practice in both form and function is key to student success.

How does **Grammar Form and Function** incorporate form and function into its approach to teaching grammar?

For each grammar point, the text follows a consistent format:

- ❖ **Presentation of Form.** The text presents the complete form, or formal rule, along with several examples for students to clearly see the model. There are also relevant photos to help illustrate the grammar point.
- ❖ **Presentation of Function.** The text explains the function of the grammar point, or how it is used, along with additional examples for reinforcement.
- ❖ **Practice.** Diverse exercises practice the form and function together. Practice moves logically from more controlled to less controlled activities.
- ❖ **Application.** Students apply the grammar point in open-ended communicative activities. **Your Turn** requires students to draw from and speak about personal experiences, and **Writing** provides a variety of writing assignments that rely on communicative group and pair discussions. **Expansion** activities in the Teacher's Manual provide additional creative, fun practice for students.

What is the purpose of the photos in the book?

Most people have a visual memory. When you see a photo aligned with a grammar point, the photo helps you remember and contextualize the grammar. The photo reinforces the learning and retention. If there were no visual image, you'd be more likely to forget the grammar point. For example, let's say you are learning the present progressive. You read the example "She is drinking a glass of water." At the same time, you are shown a photo of a girl drinking a glass of water. Later, you are more likely to recall the form of the present progressive because your mind has made a mental picture that helps you remember.

Practice

How were the grammar points selected?

We did a comprehensive review of courses at this level to ensure that all of the grammar points taught were included.

Does **Grammar Form and Function** have controlled or communicative practice?

It has both. Students practice each grammar point through controlled exercises and then move on to tackle open-ended communicative activities.

Do students have a chance to personalize the grammar?

Yes. There are opportunities to personalize the grammar in **Your Turn** and **Writing**. **Your Turn** requires students to draw from and speak about personal experiences, and **Writing** provides a variety of writing assignments that rely on communicative group and pair discussions.

Does **Grammar Form and Function** help students work toward fluency or accuracy?

Both. The exercises are purposefully designed to increase students' accuracy and enhance their fluency by practicing both form and function. Students' confidence in their accuracy helps boost their fluency.

Why does the text feature writing practice?

Grammar and writing are linked in a natural way. Specific grammar structures lend themselves to specific writing genres. In *Grammar Form and Function*, carefully devised practice helps students keep these structures in mind as they are writing.

In addition to the grammar charts, what other learning aids are in the book?

The book includes 19 pages of appendices that are designed to help the students as they complete the exercises. In addition to grammar resources such as lists of irregular verbs and spelling rules for endings, the appendices also feature useful and interesting information, including grammar terms, rules for capitalization and punctuation, writing basics, and even maps. In effect, the appendices constitute a handbook that students can use not only in grammar class, but in other classes as well.

Are there any additional practice opportunities?

Yes, there are additional exercises in the Workbook and on the Website. There are also **Expansion** activities in the Teacher's Manual that provide more open-ended (and fun!) practice for students.

Assessment

What is the role of student self-assessment in Grammar Form and Function?

Every opportunity for student self-assessment is valuable! *Grammar Form and Function* provides two Self-Tests for each unit – one at the end of each Student Book unit and another at the end of each Workbook unit. The Self-Tests build student confidence, encourage student independence as learners, and increase student competence in following standardized test formats. In addition, the Self-Tests serve as important tools for the teacher in measuring student mastery of grammar structures.

Does Grammar Form and Function offer students practice in standardized test formats?

Yes, the two Self-Tests and the Unit Quiz for each unit all utilize standardized test formats. Teachers may use the three tests in the way that best meets student, teacher, and institutional needs. For example, teachers may first assign the Self-Test in the Workbook as an untimed practice test to be taken at home. Then in the classroom, teachers may administer the Self-Test in the Student Book for a more realistic, but still informal, test-taking experience. Finally, teachers may administer the Unit Quiz from the Teacher's Manual as a more standardized timed test.

How long should each Self-Test or Unit Quiz take?

Since there is flexibility in implementing the Self-Tests and Unit Quizzes, there is also flexibility in the timing of the tests. When used for informal test-taking practice at home or in class, they may be administered as untimed tests. When administered as timed tests in class, they should take no more than 20 minutes.

How can I be sure students have mastered the grammar?

Grammar Form and Function provides a variety of tools to evaluate student mastery of the grammar. Traditional evaluation tools include the practice exercises, Self-Tests, and Unit Quizzes. To present a more complete picture of student mastery, the series also includes **Your Turn** activities and **Writing**, which illustrate how well students have internalized the grammar structures and are able to apply them in realistic tasks. Teachers can use these activities to monitor and assess students' ability to incorporate new grammatical structures into their spoken and written discourse.

Unit Format

What is the unit structure of **Grammar Form and Function**?

Consult the guide to *Grammar Form and Function* on pages VIII-XI. This walk-through provides a visual tour of a Student Book unit.

How many hours of instruction are in **Grammar Form and Function 1?**

The key to *Grammar Form and Function* is flexibility! The grammar structures in the Student Book may be taught in order, or teachers may rearrange units into an order that best meets their students' needs. To shorten the number of hours of instruction, teachers may choose not to teach all of the grammar structures, or use all of the exercises provided. On the other hand, teachers may add additional hours by assigning exercises in the Workbook or on the Website. In addition, the Teacher's Manual provides teaching suggestions and expansion activities that would add extra hours of instruction.

Ancillary Components

What can I find in the Teacher's Manual?

- ❖ Teaching tips and techniques
- ❖ Overview of each unit
- ❖ Answer keys for the Student Book and Workbook
- ❖ Expansion activities
- ❖ Culture, usage, and vocabulary notes
- ❖ Answers to frequently asked questions about the grammar structures
- ❖ Unit quizzes in a standardized test format and quiz answer keys.

How do I supplement classroom instruction with the Workbook?

The Workbook exercises can be used to add instructional hours to the course, to provide homework practice, and to reinforce and refresh the skills of students who have mastered the grammar structures. It also provides additional standardized test-taking practice.

What can students find on the Website?

Students and teachers will find a wealth of engaging listening and reading activities on the *Grammar Form and Function* Website. As with the Workbook, the Website exercises can be used to add instructional hours to the course, to provide homework practice, and to reinforce and refresh the skills of students who have mastered the grammar structures.

UNIT 8

THE FUTURE TENSE

8a The Future Tense: *Be Going To*

Jamie is hungry.

She**'s going to eat** the cookie.

AFFIRMATIVE STATEMENTS		
Subject + *Be*	*Going To*	Base Verb
I **am**		
You **are**		
He/She/It **is**	**going to**	**eat.**
We **are**		
They **are**		

NEGATIVE STATEMENTS		
Subject + *Be*	Not *Going To*	Base Verb
I **am**		
You **are**		
He/She/It **is**	**not going to**	**eat.**
We **are**		
They **are**		

YES/NO QUESTIONS			SHORT ANSWERS	
Be + Subject	*Going To*	Base verb	Affirmative	Negative
			Yes,	**No,**
Am I			you **are.**	you **aren't.**
Are you			I **am.**	I'm **not.**
Is he/she/it	going to	eat?	he/she/it **is.**	he/she/it **isn't.**
Are we			you **are.**	you **aren't.**
Are you			we **are.**	we **aren't.**
Are they			they **are.**	they **aren't.**

WH- QUESTIONS				
Wh- Word	*Be*	Subject	*Going To*	Base Verb
What				
Where				
When	are	you	going to	eat?
Why				
How				
Who*	are	you	going to	see?

Note: We often pronounce *going to* as "gonna" when we speak.
* In formal written English, the wh- word would be *whom*.

Look at those clouds!
It's going to rain soon.

1. We use *be* + *going to* + base verb to make predictions about the future. (what we know or think is going to happen very soon.)

2. We use *be* + *going to* + base verb to talk about our plans for the future.

We**'re going to buy** a house next year.

3

The Future Tense

1 Practice

Look at the photos. Then complete the sentences with *be going to* and a phrase from the list.

buy some fruit	hit the ball	pay the bill
drink a cup of coffee	order a meal	take a photo
eat an ice cream cone	paint the wall	write a check

1. Jim has a camera.

Jim is going to take

a photo .

2. Brad has a paintbrush.

_____

_____ .

3. Sue is in the supermarket.

_____

_____ .

4. Tony is in a café.

_____

_____ .

5. Mel has a checkbook and a pen.

_____

_____ .

6. Ted is in a restaurant.

_____

_____ .

4

7. Bill is in a store.

_____

_____.

8. Sue has an ice cream cone.

_____

_____.

9. Mike has a tennis racket.

_____

_____.

Practice

Complete the dialogue with forms of _be going to_. Yuko is talking to Meg about her trip to London next week.

Yuko: Guess what! I (go) <u>'m going to go</u> to London next week!
        ₁

Meg :   Lucky you! You (not/work) _____! How long
        ₂

        (stay) _____ you _____?
        ₃   ₄

Yuko: I (stay) _____ for five days. I (fly) _____ on Sunday.
        ₅   ₆

Meg: (stay) _____ you _____ in a hotel in London?
        ₇   ₈

Yuko: Yes, I _____. It's expensive, but there are so many things I
        ₉

        want to see. On Monday, I (see) _____ St. Paul's and
        ₁₀

        then I (walk) _____ in the parks. On Tuesday, I
        ₁₁

        (visit) _____ the Houses of Parliament. On Wednesday,
        ₁₂

        I (look) _____ at some museums. On Thursday,
        ₁₃

        I (shop) _____ on Oxford Street. I
        ₁₄

        (buy) _____ some English tea.
        ₁₅

Meg: I see you made plans for every day. (eat) _____ you _____ fish
        ₁₆   ₁₇

        and chips? English people eat fish and chips, you know.

Yuko: That's one thing I (not/do) _____. I don't like fish.
        ₁₈

        I (eat) _____ hamburgers as usual.
        ₁₉

Practice

Your friend is going to have a party. Ask him/her questions about it. Use the prompts to make questions. Give your own answers.

1. When/you/have the party?

   Question: _When are you going to have the party_ ?

   Answer: _On Saturday_ .

2. What kind of food/you/have?

   Question: _____?

   Answer: _____.

3. What food/you/make?

   Question: _____?

   Answer: _____.

4. What/you/wear?

   Question: _____?

   Answer: _____.

5. How many people/you/invite?

   Question: _____?

   Answer: _____.

6. Where/you/have the party?

   Question: _____?

   Answer: _____.

7. What time/the party/start?

   Question: _____?

   Answer: _____.

8. What kind of music/you/have?

   Question: _____?

   Answer: _____.

Say what you are going to do or are not going to do on the weekend.

Example:
sleep late
I'm going to sleep late.
write letters
I'm not going to write letters.

1. watch television	**5.** phone your friends	**9.** go shopping
2. clean your room	**6.** cook a meal	**10.** see a movie
3. play a sport	**7.** meet a friend	**11.** do homework
4. do the laundry	**8.** work on a computer	**12.** visit a relative

8b Future Time Expressions

Form

Jane is happy. She got a letter from Paul. He's going to come back **next Friday!** That's **in eight days!**

Next		Tomorrow		In		Other Expressions
next	week month weekend summer Friday	**tomorrow**	morning afternoon evening night	**in**	ten minutes three hours four days five weeks six months two years	**soon** **tonight** **the day after tomorrow** **a week from today/now**

We use future time expressions at the beginning or at the end of the sentence. We use a comma (,) after the time expression when it is at the beginning of the sentence.

In eight days, Paul is going to come home.
Paul is going to come home **in eight days.**

Remember: We use time expressions like *yesterday, ago,* and *last* with the past tense.

5 | Your Turn

Write about your life. Use time expressions and *be going to*.

1. Next summer, *I'm going to visit my aunt in California* .

2. In a couple of months, _____.

3. In two days, _____.

4. A week from now, _____.

5. Next Monday, _____.

6. Tomorrow evening, _____.

7. Tonight, _____.

8. Later today, _____.

9. In a few minutes, _____.

6 | Practice

Complete the sentences. Use *tomorrow, next, in, yesterday, last,* and *ago*.

1. Paul went to Los Angeles four months _____ago_____.

2. He called Janine _____ week from Los Angeles.

3. Janine got a letter from Paul two days _____.

4. Paul is going to come home _____ week.

5. He is going to be here _____ one week.

6. Janine is going to buy a gift for Paul _____.

7. Paul didn't call Janine _____.

8. Janine is going to be very happy _____ Friday.

9. Paul and Janine are going to be married _____ June.

10. They are going to be married _____ three months.

11. They decided to get married six months _____.

12. They decided to get married _____ October.

---

7 **Your Turn**

Work with a partner. Ask and answer questions with *When are you going to...?* or *When did you...?*

Example:
have dinner
You: When are you going to have dinner?
Your partner: I'm going to have dinner in two hours.

1. have dinner   3. do your homework   5. go home   7. use a computer
2. go to the store 4. call your friend   6. watch television 8. come to class

---

8c   The Future Tense: The Present Progressive as a Future Tense

Form

John **is meeting** the director in 20 minutes.
He **is seeing** the director at 11:00 this morning.

Subject + *Be*	Base Verb + *-ing*	
I'm		
You're		
He's	**meeting**	the director in 20 minutes.
She's		
We're		
They're		

Steve **is leaving** for New York in two hours.

He's at the airport now.

1. We use the present progressive to talk about future plans. We often use a time expression with the present progressive. We use the present progressive especially with verbs of movement and transportation such as *come*, *go*, *fly*, *travel*, and *leave*.

2. We can also use *be going to* for future plans.

   Steve **is going to leave** for New York in two hours.
   OR
   Steve **is leaving** for New York in two hours.

3. We cannot use the present progressive for future predictions.

   CORRECT: Look at those dark clouds! It**'s going to** rain soon.
   INCORRECT: Look at those dark clouds! It's raining soon.

8 Practice

A.

Jan is going to New York on a business trip. Look at her schedule. Write about what she is doing on Monday. Use the present progressive of the verbs in parentheses.

MONDAY	
8:45	Arrive in New York. Take a taxi to the hotel.
9:30	Leave the hotel.
10:00	Meet Tim and Donna at the office.
10:00–12:00	Work with Tim and Donna.
12:00–2:00	Have lunch with Tim, Donna, and the boss.
2:30	See Tod Cordel.
4:00	Return to the office. Work with Donna.
6:00	Go back to the hotel.
7:00	Wait for Alex in the hotel lobby. Go to dinner.
10:00	Return to the hotel. Prepare for meeting on Tuesday at 9:00.

1. (arrive) _At 8:45 she is arriving in New York_____.

2. (take) _____.

3. (leave) _____.

4. (meet) _____.

5. (work) _____.

6. (have) _____.

7. (see) _____.

8. (return) _____.

9. (go back) _____.

10. (wait for) _____.

11. (go) _____.

12. (return) _____.

13. (prepare) _____.

B.
Work with a partner. Write questions and give answers.

1. What time/arrive/in New York?

    _What time is Jan arriving in New York_____?

    _She is arriving in New York at 8:45_____.

2. Who/meet/at 10:00?

    _____?

    _____.

3. What/do/between 12:00 and 2:00?

    _____?

    _____.

4. Where/wait/for Alex?

    _____?

    _____.

5. What/do/at 10:00?

    _____?

    _____.

9 Practice

Complete the dialogue. Use the present progressive of the verbs in parentheses.

Mike: What (do) *are* you _____*doing*_____ this weekend?
                ¹   ²

Jackie: Well, I'm really very busy. Tonight I (go) _____ out to dinner with
                                                    ³

       my friend Lulu. She's great fun. We always have a good time. Then on Saturday

       morning I (take) _____ a computer class.
                              ⁴

Mike: Finally! You're learning to use a computer!

Jackie: Yes, I love it. I'm doing well, too. Then, after that, I (meet) _____
                                                                                ⁵

       my mother. We (go) _____ shopping to get my father a birthday gift.
                             ⁶

       Then, in the evening, I (have)_____ dinner with Chris. On Sunday,
                                        ⁷

       Chris and I (go) _____ to a friend's wedding. So on Sunday morning,
                          ⁸

       I (get) _____ dressed, and he (pick) _____ me up to
               ⁹   ¹⁰

       go there. He (drive) _____ there. It's a long drive. We
                            ¹¹

       (stay) _____ there for the dinner reception then we
                  ¹²

       (come) _____ back at around six. Chris (fly) _____
                   ¹³   ¹⁴

       to Boston in the evening, and I (go) _____ over to Magda's place
                                          ¹⁵

       to study English. You know we (have) _____ a test on Monday.
                                       ¹⁶

       So anyway, Mike, what (do) _____ you _____?
                               ¹⁷   ¹⁸

Mike: Oh, nothing really.

Jackie: My bus is here. See you Monday! Bye!

10 Your Turn

Work with a partner. Ask and answer the questions.

Example:
You: Where are you going after class?
Your partner: I'm going home.

Today	Tomorrow	On the weekend
where/go/after class	what/do/tomorrow	where/go/Saturday
how/get/there	where/go/evening	what/do/Sunday
what/do/this evening		

8d The Future Tense: *Will*

One day, people **will go** to the moon for vacations.

AFFIRMATIVE AND NEGATIVE STATEMENTS		
Subject	*Will (Not)*	Base Verb
I		
You	**will**	
He/She/It	**will not**	**go.**
We	**won't**	
They		

WH- QUESTIONS			
Wh- Word	*Will*	Subject	Base Verb
What			
Where		I	**do?**
When		you	**stay?**
Why	**will**	he/she/it	**know?**
How		we	**wait?**
How long		they	**see?**
Who*			

* In formal written English, the wh- word would be *whom*.

YES/NO QUESTIONS		
Will	Subject	Main Verb
Will	I	
	you	
	he	
	she	**go?**
	it	
	we	
	they	

SHORT ANSWERS	
Affirmative	Negative
Yes,	**No,**
you **will.**	you **won't.**
I/we **will.**	I/we **won't.**
he **will.**	he **won't.**
she **will.**	she **won't.**
it **will.**	it **won't.**
you **will.**	you **won't.**
they **will.**	they **won't.**

Note: Do not use contractions in affirmative short answers.
CORRECT: Yes, they will.
INCORRECT: Yes, ~~they'll.~~

Scientists **will find** a cure for cancer one day.

1. We use *will* to make predictions about the future (what we think will happen).

Those shoes are very comfortable.
I'll buy them.

2. We use *will* for the future when we decide to do something at the moment of speaking.

3. We do not use *will* for the future when plans were made before this moment.

Angie:	What are your plans for tomorrow?
Dick:	We**'re going to** drive to Disneyland.
OR:	We**'re driving** to Disneyland.
NOT:	We'll drive to Disneyland.

11 Practice

Make predictions for the year 2050. Say what you think. Use *will or won't* in the blanks.

1. People _____*will*_____ drive electric cars.

2. Everybody _____ have a computer at home.

3. People _____ carry money.

4. People _____ take vacations on the moon.

5. All people _____ speak the same language.

6. All people around the world _____ use the same currency (money).

7. People _____ find life on other planets.

8. People _____ get serious diseases like cancer.

9. Trains _____ travel very fast.

10. People _____ live to be 130 years old.

11. Men and women _____ continue to marry.

12. Children _____ go to school five days a week.

Discuss with your partner or the class.
Write three sentences with *will* or *won't* about what you think will happen.

12 Practice

Complete the conversation with forms of the present progressive, *will,* and *be going to.*

Julia: I (go) _____*am going*_____ to the supermarket right now. Do you want anything?
                          1

Leyla: Yes. Can you get some orange juice?

Julia: Sure. It's on my list, so I (get) _____ it.
                                              2

Leyla: I also wanted to pick up my photos today, but I don't have time to do it.

Julia: Don't worry. I (pick) _____ them up for you. I
                                     3
    (be) _____ back soon. (be) _____ you _____ here?
              4   5   6

Leyla: I (go) _____ to work now.
                    7

Julia: OK. I (see) _____ you later. Remember Tony and Suzy
                          8
    (come) _____ tonight.
                   9

13 Practice

Complete the telephone conversation between Steve and Dave with forms of the present progressive, *will,* and *be going to*.

Steve: Hi Dave. (go) <u>Are</u> you <u>going</u> to the picnic on Saturday?
                      ₁   ₂

Dave: I don't think I can. I (help) _____ 3 _____ Joanne move from her

apartment.

Steve: Oh no! I forgot she (move) _____ 4 _____ this weekend.

Dave: Well, (come) _____ 5 _____ you _____ 6 _____ to help?

Steve: Sure. What time (go) _____ 7 _____ you _____ 8 _____ to Joanne's apartment?

Dave: I don't know right now. I (call) _____ 9 _____ you tomorrow night,

and I (tell) _____ 10 _____ you.

Steve: OK. Someone is knocking on the door right now. I (see) _____ 11 _____

who it is. I (call) _____ 12 _____ you right back. Bye.

Dave. OK. Bye.

14 Your Turn

Ask and answer the questions with a partner.

Example:
You: What will you do after this course?
Your partner: I think I'll take the next level.

1. Where will you be at 6:00 tomorrow evening?
2. Where will you go on the weekend?
3. Where will you go for your next vacation?
4. When will you buy a car/a new car?

8e *May, Might,* and *Will*

Oh no! I'm late!
I **may** miss my flight.

AFFIRMATIVE STATEMENTS			NEGATIVE STATEMENTS		
Subject	*May/Might*	Base Verb	Subject	*May/Might Not*	Base Verb
I			I		
You			You		
He			He		
She	**may**	**go.**	She	**may not**	**go.**
It	**might**		It	**might not**	
We			We		
They			They		

Notes: Contractions for *may* or *might* are very rare.
We don't usually use *may* or *might* in yes/no questions.

1. We use *may* or *might* to talk about something that is possible now or in the future.

   I **may/might** go to Mexico next year.

   You **may/might** have a problem with your computer.

   May and *might* have the same meaning. They both express a possibility.

2. We can also use *may* (but not *might*) to give, refuse, or ask for permission.

   You **may** use a dictionary during the test.

   You **may** not go early.

   May I use your phone?

3. We use *will, be going to,* or the present progressive when we are certain about something. We use *may/might* when we are not certain.

   I **may** be late. (It's possible.)

   I**'ll** be late. (It's certain.)

   I**'m going to** be late. (It's certain.)

---

[15] Practice

A friend is traveling around the world. Use *will* if you are certain. Use *may* or *might* if you are not certain.

1. Friend: I'm going to Boston this winter.

   You: Take warm clothes. It ____*will*____ be cold. It's always cold there in winter.

2. Friend: I'm going to Los Angeles in the summer.

   You: Take your shorts and light clothes. It _____ be hot. It's always hot

   there in the summer.

3. Friend: I want to walk around New York at night.

   You: Be careful. It _____ be dangerous. People sometimes get hurt.

4. Friend: In June, I'm going to Bangkok, in Thailand.

   You: Take an umbrella. It _____ be rainy. It always rains there in June.

5. Friend: I'm going to stay in Tokyo for a month.

   You: Take a lot of money. It _____ be expensive. Tokyo is always expensive.

6. Friend: I'm flying from New York to Sydney, Australia.

You: It's a long trip. Take a book with you. You _____ get bored.

7. Friend: I want to go to Rio de Janeiro for the Carnival.

You: Make a hotel reservation. It _____ be crowded. It's always crowded then.

8. Friend: I'm going to Africa to see wild animals.

You: Take some medicine with you. You _____ get sick. People sometimes get sick when they travel there.

16 Practice

Underline the correct verb.

1. I'<u>m going</u>/**might go** to New York next week. I have my ticket already.

2. I **may stay**/**'m staying** at the Ambassador Hotel. I have a reservation for next week.

3. I'**ll go**/**may go** to New Jersey or perhaps to Boston from New York.

4. I **won't spend**/**may not spend** much time out of New York because my work will keep me too busy.

5. I'**ll finish**/**might finish** my work in New York before Friday of next week. My return flight is on that day.

6. I'**ll see**/**might see** a show on Broadway. I'm not sure.

7. It's my birthday on Wednesday. I **may celebrate**/**will celebrate** it in New York!

8. I'**ll go**/**may go** to an expensive restaurant. I'm not sure.

17 Your Turn

Tell the class five things you may or might do in five years. Use these ideas or your own.

Example:
I might go to another country, for example, to China.

1. go to another country
2. go to college
3. get married
4. get a job
5. stay with your family

8f Future Time Clauses with *Before, After,* and *When*

She**'ll wear** her new suit when
she **goes** to the interview.

1. A future time clause can begin with *before, after,* and *when*.

2. When a time clause refers to the future, the verb is in the simple present tense.

TIME CLAUSE				MAIN CLAUSE		
Simple Present				Future		
Before	I	**go**	to bed,	I	**will do**	my homework.
When	she	**goes**	to the interview,	she	**will wear**	her new suit.
After	we	**finish**	the test,	we	**will go**	home.

CORRECT: Before I **go** to bed, I will do my homework.
INCORRECT: Before I ~~will go~~ to bed, I will do my homework.

1. We can put the time clause before or after the main clause. They both have the same meaning.

   She'll wear her new suit **when she goes to the interview.**
   When she goes to the interview, she'll wear her new suit.

2. When the time clause comes first, we put a comma (,) after the time clause.

18 Practice

Laura has an interview tomorrow. Underline the time clauses in the sentences about her.

1. She'll have breakfast <u>before she goes to the interview</u>.

2. Before she leaves home, she'll take some important letters with her.

3. She'll try and relax before she goes to the interview.

4. When she meets the interviewer, she'll smile.

5. When the interviewer asks questions, she'll answer all of them.

6. After the interview, she'll call her mother.

7. She'll meet her friend after the interview.

8. When they meet, they'll talk about the interview.

9. She'll be worried before she gets the news about her job.

10. When she gets the job, she'll celebrate.

19 Practice

Jim and Paula Newley are planning a trip to Istanbul, Turkey. Complete the sentences with the words in parentheses.

1. We (change) ___*will change*___ some money before we leave.

2. We (make) _____ a list of all the interesting places before we leave.

3. When we (get) _____ there, we'll stay at the Hilton hotel.

4. After we see the city, we (visit) _____ the museums.

5. When we stay in Istanbul, we (not, go) _____ to other cities.

6. We won't have time to see everything before we (leave) _____.

7. We'll go to the bazaar after we (visit) _____ the museums.

8. When we go to the bazaar, we (buy) _____ a rug.

9. When we walk around the bazaar, we (take) _____ photos.

10. When we (stay) _____ in Istanbul, we won't need a car.

11. We'll take a taxi when we (want) _____ to go somewhere.

12. Before we leave Istanbul, we (get) _____ lots of souvenirs.

[20] Your Turn

Work with a partner. Ask and answer the questions.

Example:

You: What are you doing today before you take the test?

Your partner: I'm going to get a good night's sleep before I take the test.

1. What are you going to do before you eat dinner?

2. What are you going to do after you eat dinner?

3. What are you going to eat when you have dinner?

8g Future Conditional Sentences

If the weather **is** nice tomorrow,
we**'ll go** fishing.

1. A conditional sentence has a main clause and a dependent clause that starts with *if*. We call this kind of dependent clause an *if* clause.

2. In future conditional sentences, we use the simple present in an *if* clause to express future time. We use a future tense in the main clause.

IF CLAUSE			MAIN CLAUSE		
		Present		Future	
If	I	**have time,**	I	**will see**	you.
If	you	**don't hurry,**	you	**will be**	late.
If	she	**gets the job,**	she	**is going to buy**	a car.
If	it	**is sunny,**	we	**will go**	fishing.
If	we	**leave now,**	we	**will get there**	in time.
If	they	**don't go today,**	they	**will miss**	it.

3. An *if* clause can come before or after the main clause. The meaning is the same.

> If the weather is nice tomorrow, we**'ll** go fishing.
> We**'ll** go fishing if the weather is nice tomorrow.

CORRECT: If I **have** time tomorrow, I will visit you.
INCORRECT: If I ~~will have~~ time tomorrow, I will visit you.

4. When the *if* clause comes first, we put a comma (,) after it.

We use future conditional sentences to say that one situation in the future depends on another situation.

> If I have time tomorrow, I will visit you. (I may or may not have time, so I may or may not visit you.)

> If she sees Tony, she'll invite him to the party.

21 Practice

Tim is going to be away from home. His mother is worried about him. Match the sentence parts. Then write sentences below.

	A		**B**
_c_ **1.**	go out without a coat	**a.**	be hungry
____ **2.**	lie in the sun	**b.**	not pass your exam
____ **3.**	don't eat breakfast	**c.**	catch a cold
____ **4.**	eat too many French fries	**d.**	call home
____ **5.**	don't study hard	**e.**	not tired the next day
____ **6.**	get lonely	**f.**	get sunburned
____ **7.**	go to bed early	**g.**	miss class
____ **8.**	get sick	**h.**	get fat

1. _If you go out without a coat, you'll catch a cold_ .

2. _____ .

3. _____ .

4. _____ .

5. _____ .

6. _____ .

7. _____ .

8. _____ .

22   Practice

Complete the sentences with the correct future tense form of the verb in parentheses. Sometimes two answers are possible.

1. What are we doing this Saturday? Well, if the weather is nice, we (go)

   _____*will go / are going to go*_____ to the park.

2. If it (rain) _____ , we'll stay at home.

3. If we stay home, we (watch) _____ television.

4. We (watch) _____ a video if there's

   nothing good on television.

5. I (not, cook) _____ if we stay home.

6. I (order) _____ a pizza if we eat at home.

7. If the pizza is expensive, Tony (make) _____

   pasta.

8. He (cook) _____ pasta if there is no food.

9. If Tony cooks, he (cook) _____ pasta.

   He only knows how to cook pasta.

10. If we go to the park, we (play) _____ baseball.

11. If we (get) _____ tired, we

    _____ (sit) on the grass.

12. If we (go) _____ to the park, we

    (have) _____ a picnic.

13. I (go) _____ to the store to get some

    things if we (have) _____ a picnic.

14. If the weather (be) _____ hot, we

    (take) _____ the ice chest.

15. If we (go) _____ to the park, we

(not, drive) _____. We'll walk.

16. We (have) _____ a good time if we

(go) _____ to the park. We always do.

- Work with a partner or a group. Ask and answer the questions.

Example:
You: What are you going to do if it rains tonight?
Your partner: If it rains tonight, I'm going to stay home and watch television.

1. What will you do if the weather is nice this weekend?
2. What will you do if the weather is cold?
3. What will you do if there is no class tomorrow?
4. What are you going to do if you do not have homework tonight?

8h   The Simple Present Tense with Time Clauses and *If* Clauses

Form

When you **get** thirsty, you **drink** water.

We sometimes use the simple present in the dependent clause (the *if* clause or the time clause) and also in the main clause.

Time Clause/*If* Clause	Main Clause
Before the teacher **walks** into the classroom,	the students **make** a lot of noise.
After I **get up**,	I usually **have** a cup of tea.
When you **get** thirsty,	you **drink** water.
If you **water** plants,	they **grow.**

If the temperature **falls** below zero, water **turns** to ice.

We use the simple present in both the dependent clause and the main clause when:

1. The action is habitual. (It happens all the time.)
2. We are expressing something that is always true.

   If the temperature **falls** below zero, water **turns** to ice. (Always true.)

   When I **go** to Mexico, I usually **stay** with my grandmother. (Habitual action.)
   BUT
   When I **go** to Mexico next summer, I **will stay** with my grandmother.
   (Specific action in future.)

24 Practice

Match the sentence parts. Then write sentences.

	A		**B**
_c_ **1.**	don't water plants	**a.**	it goes bad
2.	put food in the refrigerator	**b.**	you get gray
3.	put water in the freezer	**c.**	they die
4.	walk in the rain	**d.**	it stays fresh
5.	mix black and white	**e.**	it turns into ice
6.	don't put milk in the refrigerator	**f.**	you get wet

1. *If you don't water plants, they die* _____.

2. _____.

3. _____.

4. _____.

5. _____.

6. _____.

25 Practice

Complete the sentences with main clauses about you.

1. If I have a headache, _I take an aspirin_____.

2. If I eat too much, _____.

3. If I don't sleep, _____.

4. If I miss my class, _____.

5. If I get very angry, _____.

6. When I am sad, _____.

7. When I am happy, _____.

8. When I have a test, _____.

26 Practice

Complete the sentences with the correct form of the verb in parentheses.

1. Julia works in an office from 9:00 to 5:00. When she has some extra work, she (stay) _____stays_____ until 6:00.

2. If she has a lot of work tomorrow, she (stay) _____ until 8:00.

3. If she's at the office, she usually (see) _____ Terry at lunchtime.

4. If the weather is nice, they usually (go) _____ out for lunch.

5. If she (see) _____ Terry tomorrow, she (tell) _____ him she's very busy.

6. Julia (not, go) _____ out for lunch tomorrow if she's very busy.

7. When she gets hungry tomorrow, she (have) _____ a sandwich at her desk.

8. She usually (like) _____ to have a salad or a bowl of soup when she goes out with Terry.

9. Julia usually gets tired when she (work) _____ on the computer all day.

10. Tomorrow, she (go) _____ to meetings before she works on the computer.

11. When she (come) _____ home tomorrow, it (be) _____ about 8:30.

12. She usually (make) _____ dinner when she (come) _____ home.

13. If she (be) _____ tired tomorrow, she (not, make) _____ dinner.

14. She (buy) _____ a sandwich before she (come) _____ home from work tomorrow.

15. Julia usually (turn) _____ on her computer after she (have) _____ dinner.

16. Tomorrow, Julia (not, turn) _____ on her computer after she (have) _____ dinner.

17. After she (have) _____ dinner tomorrow, she (go) _____ to bed.

18. If she (work) _____ like this all year, Julia (ask) _____ for more money from her boss.

27 Your Turn

Work with a partner. Ask and answer the questions.

Example:
You: What do you usually do before you go to bed?
Your partner: I usually read before I go to bed.

1. What do you usually do before you go to bed?
2. What do you usually do when you get up in the morning?
3. What are you going to do when you get up on Sunday morning?
4. What do you usually do when you get paid or get money?
5. What are you going to do when you get money the next time?
6. What do you usually do on Sundays if the weather is nice?
7. What are you going to do on Sunday if the weather is nice?

Write a paragraph about future plans.

Step 1.   Work with a partner. A friend is coming to your town/city for three days. It is his/her first visit. Make a list of four good places to go.

1. _____   **3.** _____

2. _____   **4.** _____

Step 2.   Plan your three days. Where are you going to go first, second, third, and last? Your friend is arriving at 4:00 at the airport near your town. Ask your partner questions like these. Write the answers to the questions.

1.   Are you going to meet your friend at the airport?
2.   Where are you going to take him/her after that?
3.   What are you going to do that evening? Why?
4.   What are you going to do on Saturday?
5.   What are you going to do if the weather is bad?
6.   What will you do on Sunday?
7.   How will you get there?
8.   What special food will you give your friend to eat?
9.   What will you do if he/she doesn't like it?
10. Where will you go on Monday? Your friend is going back at 6:00 on Monday.

Step 3.   Rewrite your answers in paragraph form. For more writing guidelines, see pages 190-195.

Step 4.   Write a title in three to five words, for example, "My Friend Visits Chicago."

Step 5.   Evaluate your paragraph.

Checklist

_____   Did you indent the first line?
_____   Did you give your paragraph a title?
_____   Did you capitalize the title correctly?
_____   Did you use verb tenses correctly?

Step 6.   Work with a partner to edit your paragraph. Correct spelling, punctuation, vocabulary, and grammar.

Step 7.   Write your final copy.

SELF-TEST

A **Choose the best answer, A, B, C, or D, to complete the sentence. Mark your answer by darkening the oval with the same letter.**

1. When I go to London, I _____ Buckingham Palace.

    A. am visiting
    B. going visit
    C. am going to visit
    D. will visiting

    Ⓐ Ⓑ Ⓒ Ⓓ

2. What _____ on the weekend?

    A. are you going to do
    B. are you going
    C. you are going to do
    D. you doing

    Ⓐ Ⓑ Ⓒ Ⓓ

3. Paul and Jane _____ married next year.

    A. going to
    B. are going to be
    C. will to be
    D. being

    Ⓐ Ⓑ Ⓒ Ⓓ

4. A: Would you like to come to our place this Thursday?
    B: OK. I _____ at 7:00.

    A. am going to come
    B. 'll come
    C. am coming
    D. will coming

    Ⓐ Ⓑ Ⓒ Ⓓ

5. Oh no! Look at that car! It _____!

    A. is crashing
    B. will crash
    C. is going to crash
    D. crashes

    Ⓐ Ⓑ Ⓒ Ⓓ

6. In twenty years, most people _____ electric cars.

    A. are driving
    B. will drive
    C. going drive
    D. is going to drive

    Ⓐ Ⓑ Ⓒ Ⓓ

7. I will be worried before I _____ to the interview.

    A. will go
    B. go
    C. am going
    D. may go

    Ⓐ Ⓑ Ⓒ Ⓓ

8. If you study hard tonight, you _____ your math test tomorrow.

    A. pass
    B. are passing
    C. will pass
    D. passing

    Ⓐ Ⓑ Ⓒ Ⓓ

9. If you mix blue and yellow, you _____ green.

    A. are getting
    B. will be get
    C. get
    D. might to get

    Ⓐ Ⓑ Ⓒ Ⓓ

10. After I get up, I usually _____ a shower.

    A. am taking
    B. am going to take
    C. will take
    D. take

    Ⓐ Ⓑ Ⓒ Ⓓ

B Find the underlined word or phrase, A, B, C, or D, that is incorrect. Mark your answer by darkening the oval with the same letter.

1. <u>How</u> <u>will</u> <u>be jobs</u> different in <u>the</u> future?
A   B   C   D

Ⓐ Ⓑ Ⓒ Ⓓ

2. In the United States, you <u>leave</u> a tip
A

when <u>you</u> <u>having</u> dinner <u>in a restaurant</u>.
    B   C   D

Ⓐ Ⓑ Ⓒ Ⓓ

3. If you <u>will heat</u> <u>water</u> to 212 degrees
        A   B

Fahrenheit, <u>it</u> <u>boils</u>.
         C   D

Ⓐ Ⓑ Ⓒ Ⓓ

4. <u>In twenty years</u>, people <u>will</u> <u>to</u> <u>visit</u>
   A   B   C   D

other planets.

Ⓐ Ⓑ Ⓒ Ⓓ

5. The next TOEFL test <u>is</u> <u>going to</u> <u>be</u> <u>last</u>
               A   B   C   D

June.

Ⓐ Ⓑ Ⓒ Ⓓ

6. In the future, <u>men</u> and <u>women</u> <u>will be</u>
            A   B   C

<u>continue</u> to marry.
D

Ⓐ Ⓑ Ⓒ Ⓓ

7. If sharks <u>do not</u> <u>move</u> all the time, <u>they</u>
         A   B   C

<u>will be</u> die.
D

Ⓐ Ⓑ Ⓒ Ⓓ

8. If plants <u>won't</u> <u>get</u> water, <u>they</u> <u>die</u>.
        A   B   C   D

Ⓐ Ⓑ Ⓒ Ⓓ

9. You <u>need</u> <u>a passport</u> when you <u>will travel</u>
     A   B   C

to <u>other countries</u>.
   D

Ⓐ Ⓑ Ⓒ Ⓓ

10. Before people <u>will get</u> on a plane,
             A

<u>their bags</u> <u>go</u> through <u>an X-ray</u> machine
   B   C   D

for security.

Ⓐ Ⓑ Ⓒ Ⓓ

32

UNIT 9

QUANTITY AND DEGREE WORDS

9a *All Of, Almost All Of, Most Of,* and *Some Of*

All of the people in the photo are men.
Almost all of them are wearing jackets.
Most of them are sitting.
Some of them are standing.

1. We use *all of, almost all of, most of,* and *some of* to show quantity.

All of							
Almost all of							
Most of							
Some of							

2. We use *the* plus a plural count noun or a noncount noun after these expressions. We can also use a pronoun.

   All of **the computers** are old. (Plural noun)
   All of **the information** is correct. (Noncount noun)
   All of **it** is correct. (Pronoun)

3. With these quantity words, the verb can be singular or plural. The noun tells you which one.

   All of the **books** are dictionaries.   (*Books* is plural, so the verb is plural.)
   All of the **cake** is here.   (*Cake* is singular, so the verb is singular.)
   Some of the **water** is in the glass.   (*Water* is singular, so the verb is singular.)
   Some of the **girls** are young.   (*Girls* is plural, so the verb is plural.)

1 Practice

Look at the old photo and complete the sentences with *all of the, almost all of the, most of the,* and *some of the*.

1. _All of the people_ are men.
2. _____ are wearing hats.
3. _____ are wearing a shirt and tie.
4. _____ are wearing suits.
5. _____ are sitting on the grass.
6. _____ are standing.
7. _____ are wearing jackets.
8. _____ are looking at the camera.

2 Practice

Look at another photo and complete the sentences as in Practice 1.

1. _All of the people_ are sitting.
2. _____ are wearing hats.

3. _____ are women.

4. _____ are wearing white.

5. _____ are holding something.

6. _____ are looking at the camera.

7. _____ are wearing dresses.

8. _____ are young girls.

3 Practice

Mario's Restaurant. Circle the correct verb.

Mario's Restaurant
Cucina Italiana

1223 East Street Brookford Massachussets 01201

Telephone: 518 580 3543

1. All of the food ((is)/are) delicious.

2. All of the dishes (come/comes) with a salad.

3. Most of the wines (is/are) Italian.

4. Most of the dishes (is/are) not expensive.

5. Almost all of the dishes (have/has) pasta with them.

6. Some of the servers (is/are) Italian.

7. All of the music (is/are) Italian.

8. Almost all of the furniture (is/are) Italian.

9. All of the fish (is/are) very fresh.

10. Some of the pizzas (is/are) wonderful.

4 Your Turn

Write about the students in your class. Use _all of, almost all of, most of,_ and _some of._

1. _Some of them_ _____ have dark hair.

2. _____ wear glasses.

3. _____ have dictionaries.

4. _____ are using this grammar book.

5. _____ have a bag.

6. _____ are over 18 years old.

7. _____ have a lot of homework.

8. _____ live with their parents.

9b *Every*

Every woman is smiling.
Every woman is a runner.
Every woman has a medal.
Every woman is a winner.

1. We use *every* plus a singular count noun with a singular verb. *Every* means *all*.

   Every runner **has** a number.

2. *Every* plus a singular noun means the same thing as *all of the* with a plural noun.

   Every runner was fast. = **All of the** runners were fast.

3. We do not use *every* with plural nouns, noncount nouns, or pronouns. We use *all of (the)* with them.

   INCORRECT: ~~Every~~ students passed the test.
   INCORRECT: ~~Every~~ furniture is new.
   INCORRECT: ~~Every~~ them worked very hard.

---

5 Practice

Rewrite each sentence with *every*.

1. All of the classrooms have a number.

   Every classroom has a number _____ .

2. All of the people in this school are from my country.

   _____ .

3. All of the teachers speak excellent English.

_____.

4. All of the teachers give a lot of homework.

_____.

5. All of the students in this class are learning English.

_____.

6. All of the students have a grammar book.

_____.

7. All of the units in the book have a test.

_____.

8. All of the tests have 20 questions.

_____.

9. All of the questions have four answers.

_____.

10. All of the questions are interesting.

_____.

6 Your Turn

Think of a game you play at home or outside as a sports activity. Describe the game to the class. The class guesses the game.

Example:
Every team has eleven players. The two teams wear different colors.
Every player has a number. Only the goalkeeper can touch the ball with his hands.
What is the game?

9c *Very* and *Too*

Jan: It's **very** cold today.

Kelly: Yes, it is. It's **too** cold for a picnic.

1. We use *very* and *too* before adjectives.

2. *Very* adds emphasis. It makes the word that comes after it stronger.

   It is cold. It is **very** cold.

3. *Too* shows there is a problem.

   Rosa is young. She is **too** young to drive. (She cannot drive.)

It is **very** cold today.   It's **too** cold to have a picnic. (We cannot have a picnic.)
He is **very** busy.   He is **too** busy to go. (He cannot go.)

---

7 Practice

Match the sentences.

A	B
_h_ **1.** Tony drives very fast.	**a.** I want to go there again.
____ **2.** He drinks too much coffee.	**b.** We can't go for a picnic in this weather.
____ **3.** It's too cold.	**c.** I can't go to work.
____ **4.** This exam is very hard.	**d.** I can't lift it.
____ **5.** The book is very interesting.	**e.** I will study hard and pass it.
____ **6.** The island was very beautiful.	**f.** He can't sleep at night.
____ **7.** This suitcase is too heavy.	**g.** I want to finish reading it this week.
____ **8.** I have a bad cold.	**h.** I don't worry because he's a good driver.

8 Practice

Look at the pictures. Then answer the questions. Use the words in the list.

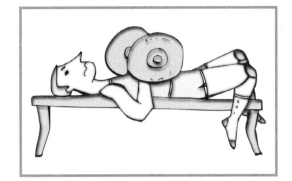 

small   heavy   hot   sleepy

1. Why can't he lift the weight?   *He can't lift it because it is too heavy*   .

2. Why can't he wear the hat?   _____.

3. Why can't she finish her homework?   _____.

4. Why can't they eat the pizza?   _____.

9 Practice

Complete the sentences with *too* or *very* and an adjective from the list.

difficult	fresh	small	tired
expensive	intelligent	sweet	young

1. Julia: That jacket is beautiful, and it's *very expensive*   .

   Pam: Are you going to buy it?

   Julia: Yes, I am.

2. Berta: Do you like our new teacher?

   Mario: Yes, I do. She's an excellent teacher, and she's _____.

3. Sue: I didn't like that cake.

    Pam: What was wrong?

    Sue: It was _____.

4. Louis: Does your sister drive?

    Maria: No, she doesn't. She's only 13. She's _____.

5. Jo: Do you want to play tennis with us this afternoon?

    Karen: I'm _____, but I think I will. Thanks.

6. Mel: Can you read this tiny writing?

    Jim: Sorry, I can't read it without my glasses. It's _____.

7. Chris: Can you help me with this statistics problem?

    Jan: Sorry, I can't. It's _____.

8. Lisa: Did you like the new fish restaurant yesterday?

    Mike: Yes, I did. The fish was _____.

---

10 Your Turn

Can you do these things? Answer with *too*. You may use the words in the list.

    heavy   high   cold   fast   difficult

1. Can you lift a piano?

    No, I can't. It's too heavy .

2. Can you learn English grammar in one week?

    _____.

3. Can you touch the ceiling?

    _____.

4. Can you live in Antarctica?

    _____.

5. Can you run five miles in one minute?

    _____.

9d *Too Many* and *Too Much*

There are **too many** cars
and **too much** noise.

1. We often use *too* with *much* and *many* to talk about quantities.

2. We use *too many* before count nouns. We use *too much* before noncount nouns.

The teacher gave us **too much** homework.
We have **too many** exercises to do.

|| Practice

Some people don't like big cities. Complete with *too much* or *too many*.

1. There is _____*too much*_____ crime.

2. There are _____ cars.

3. There is _____ traffic.

4. There are _____ tall buildings.

5. There are _____ people.

6. There is _____ pollution.

7. There is _____ noise.

8. There is _____ trash.

12 Practice

Mr. Lang had a party yesterday. Complete with *too much* or *too many*.

1. Mr. Lang spent _____*too much*_____ money.

2. There were _____ guests and _____ food.

3. There were _____ flowers everywhere.

4. There were _____ drinks.

5. There were _____ sandwiches.

6. There was _____ fruit.

7. There was _____ meat.

8. There was _____ fish.

9. There were _____ cakes.

10. There were _____ waiters.

13 Your Turn

A.
Work with a partner. Say six things about your school. Use *too much* or *too many* and words from the list.

homework   mistakes   noise   rules   students   time

Example:
We don't have too much time in a test.

B.
Now write sentences about your school using *too much* or *too many*.

1. _____.

2. _____.

3. _____.

4. _____.

5. _____.

6. _____.

9e   *Too* + Adjective + Infinitive;
Too + Adjective + *For* + Noun/Pronoun + Infinitive

He's **too small** to wear the clothes.
The clothes are **too big** for him to wear.

Subject	Verb	*Too*	Adjective	Infinitive	
I	am			**tired**	**to study.**
John	is	**too**		**sick**	**to work.**
The weather	is			**cold**	**to play tennis.**

Subject	Verb	*Too*	Adjective	*For* + Noun/Pronoun	Infinitive
The coat	is		**expensive**	for Jane	to buy.
The clothes	are	**too**	**big**	for him	to wear.
It	is		**heavy**	for her	to carry.

1. We use *too* + adjective with an infinitive after it.

2. We can also use *too* + adjective + *for* + noun/pronoun + infinitive.

   It is **too cold to have** a picnic. (*too* + adjective + infinitive)
   The clothes are **too big for him to wear.** (*too* + adjective + *for* + pronoun + infinitive)

14 Practice

Make one sentence from the two sentences. Use *too* and the infinitive.

1. I am tired. I can't drive.

   I am too tired to drive   .

2. This room is small. It isn't comfortable.

   _____ .

3. This computer is old. It doesn't work well.

   _____ .

4. Peter is sleepy. He can't study.

   _____ .

5. Janet is busy. She can't go.

   _____ .

6. The children are excited. They can't sleep.

   _____ .

15 Practice

Sandy went to stay with her uncle, Ned, but she didn't like it. Use *too* + adjective + *for* (someone) + infinitive to write sentences with the same meaning.

1. The room was cold. She couldn't sit in it.

   The room was too cold for her to sit in   .

2. The room was dark. She couldn't read.

   _____ .

3. The TV movie was boring. She couldn't watch it.

   _____ .

4. The bed was hard. She couldn't sleep in it.

   _____ .

5. The tea was strong. She couldn't drink it.

   _____ .

6. The dinner was greasy. She couldn't eat it.

   _____ .

7. The weather was stormy. She couldn't go out.

   _____ .

8. The bathroom was cold. She couldn't take a shower.

   _____ .

9f Adjective + *Enough*

The little girl is not **old enough** to talk.

Subject	Verb	(Not)	Adjective	Enough	
I	am		old		to drive.
He	is	(not)	tall	**enough**	to play basketball.
They	are		rich		to buy the house.

1. We put *enough* after an adjective.

   I am old **enough**. (adjective + *enough*)

2. *Enough* means sufficient. It has a positive meaning. It means something is possible.

   He is old **enough** to drive.

3. *Not* + adjective + *enough* means not sufficient. It has a negative meaning. It means something is not possible.

   He is **not** tall **enough** to reach the shelf.

16 Practice

Mrs. Parkway complains about everything. She goes to a restaurant and complains.
Write sentences using the words in parentheses and *too* or *enough*.

1. The chair is (uncomfortable). It is not (comfortable).

   The chair is too uncomfortable. It is not comfortable enough   .

2. The water is (hot). It is not (cold).

   _____.

3. The soup is (warm). It is not (cool).

   _____.

4. The server is (slow). He is not (fast).

   _____.

5. The server is (rude). She is not (polite).

   _____.

6. The plate is (dirty). It is not (clean).

   _____.

7. The bread is (old). It is not (fresh).

   _____.

8. The portion is (small). It is not (large).

   _____.

9. The coffee is (weak). It is not (strong).

   _____.

10. The table is (small). It is not (big).

   _____.

11. The meat is (tough). It is not (tender).

   _____.

12. The meal is (expensive). It is not (cheap).

   _____.

Quantity and Degree Words

9g *Enough* + Noun

We don't have **enough** chairs.
We have **enough** coffee, but we
don't have **enough** cups.

We can use *enough* + noun. *Enough* comes before a noun.

I can't buy a car. I don't have **enough** money.
The house is nice, but there aren't **enough** windows.

---

17 Practice

Ted had a party yesterday, but people were not happy. Complete the sentences with
enough + a word from the list.

chairs	food	light	room
drinks	glasses	money	time

1. Ted had only a little time to plan the party. He didn't have __*enough time*__ .

2. People were hungry. There wasn't _____.

3. People were standing. They had no place to sit down. There weren't _____.

4. There were twenty people and only two bottles of juice. There weren't _____.

5. There were only two glasses for twenty people. There weren't _____.

6. There were twenty people in a very small room. There wasn't _____.

7. Ted did not spend much money. He didn't have _____ to spend.

8. It was very dark. There wasn't _____ in the room.

18 Practice

Complete Janet's sentences about her party with *enough* + word from the list.

food   time   people   soda   CDs

1. Did I invite __*enough people*__ ?

2. Do I have _____ for people to eat?

3. Do I have _____ to get ready?

4. Is there _____ to drink?

5. Are there _____ to listen to?

19 Practice

Write questions and answers using the prompts below.

1. time/to go to a movie

   Question: *Do you have enough time to go to a movie* ?

   Answer: *No, I don't have enough time to go to a movie* .

2. money/to buy a CD

   Question: _____ ?

   Answer: _____ .

3. gas/to drive to New York

   Question: _____ ?

   Answer: _____ .

4. eggs/to make an omelet

   Question: _____ ?

   Answer: _____ .

5. bread/to make six sandwiches

   Question: _____ ?

   Answer: _____ .

20 Your Turn

Make sentences about your class. Use *enough* and a word from the list.

Example:
There is enough light in our classroom.

light   chairs   students   tests   homework   time

WRITING: Describe a Place

Write about your city or town.

Step 1. Work with a partner. Talk about your city or town. Talk about crime, traffic, buildings, and people who work in the city. Make sentences with the following words and phrases.

most of	very	enough
all of	too	not enough
some of	too much	
every	too many	

Example:

My city is very beautiful. Most of the offices are downtown.
Almost all of the people take the bus or subway to the city because...

Step 2. Write your sentences.

Step 3. Rewrite your sentences in paragraph form. For more writing guidelines, see pages 190-195.

Step 4. Write a title in three to five words, for example, "My City and Its Problems."

Step 5. Evaluate your work.

Checklist

_____   Did you indent the first line?
_____   Did you give your paragraph a title?
_____   Did you use capital letters correctly?
_____   Did you use verb tenses correctly?

Step 6. Work with a partner to edit your paragraph. Correct spelling, punctuation, vocabulary, and grammar.

Step 7. Write your final copy.

SELF-TEST

A. Choose the best answer, A, B, C, or D, to complete the sentence. Mark your answer by darkening the oval with the same letter.

1. I love Paris. It's a _____ city.

   A. very beautiful   (A) (B) (C) (D)
   B. beautiful enough
   C. too beautiful
   D. enough beautiful

2. We don't _____ to finish the test.

   A. have enough time   (A) (B) (C) (D)
   B. time have enough
   C. time enough have
   D. enough have time

3. She isn't _____ to drive.

   A. enough old   (A) (B) (C) (D)
   B. old enough
   C. enough age
   D. old is enough

4. I have _____ tonight.

   A. too many homeworks   (A) (B) (C) (D)
   B. too many homework
   C. too much homework
   D. very much homeworks

5. The movie was _____ . I want to see it again.

   A. too very funny   (A) (B) (C) (D)
   B. enough funny
   C. funny enough
   D. very funny

6. This homework is _____. I can't do it.

   A. difficult enough   (A) (B) (C) (D)
   B. too difficult
   C. difficult very
   D. enough difficult

7. Tom doesn't study _____ to pass his exams.

   A. hard enough   (A) (B) (C) (D)
   B. hard very
   C. enough hard
   D. too hard

8. He doesn't _____ to make a pizza.

   A. have enough flour   (A) (B) (C) (D)
   B. enough flour have
   C. have very flour
   D. have too flour

9. I can't drink this tea. It _____.

   A. isn't enough cool   (A) (B) (C) (D)
   B. is enough cool
   C. isn't cool enough
   D. isn't cool very

10. Give yourself _____ and you can do it.

    A. time enough   (A) (B) (C) (D)
    B. enough time
    C. too time
    D. very time

B Find the underlined word or phrase, A, B, C, or D, that is incorrect. Mark your answer by darkening the oval with the same letter.

1. An elephant eats about five tons of food
    A   B   C

    every days.
          D

    Ⓐ Ⓑ Ⓒ Ⓓ

2. Almost of the seas in the world have fish
    A   B   C

    in them.
       D

    Ⓐ Ⓑ Ⓒ Ⓓ

3. All of the players has numbers and names
                 A   B

    on their shirts.
       C   D

    Ⓐ Ⓑ Ⓒ Ⓓ

4. Every state in the United States have its
    A   B   C   D

    own state flag.

    Ⓐ Ⓑ Ⓒ Ⓓ

5. Almost all of the restaurants in the city
    A   B

    accepts credit cards.
    C   D

    Ⓐ Ⓑ Ⓒ Ⓓ

6. Most of the country in Europe now use
         A   B   C   D

    the Euro currency.

    Ⓐ Ⓑ Ⓒ Ⓓ

7. Every flower have its own smell.
    A   B   C   D

    Ⓐ Ⓑ Ⓒ Ⓓ

8. Every students in this class is learning
    A   B   C   D

    English.

    Ⓐ Ⓑ Ⓒ Ⓓ

9. Most people are not enough tall to be
         A   B   C

    basketball players.
                D

    Ⓐ Ⓑ Ⓒ Ⓓ

10. A boy of fourteen is not enough old to
    A   B

    drive a car.
    C   D

    Ⓐ Ⓑ Ⓒ Ⓓ

UNIT 10

OBJECTS AND PRONOUNS

10a Object Pronouns

This is a picture of my brother and **me.**
I like **him** very much.

Many sentences in English have a subject, a verb, and an object.

Noun Subject	Verb	Noun Object	Pronoun Subject	Verb	Pronoun Object
John	likes	**rice.**	**He**	likes	**it.**
Mike and Rosie	love	**their children.**	**They**	love	**them.**

1. The subject can be a noun: a person, a place, or a thing (*Mike, a restaurant, a movie*).

2. The subject can also be a pronoun (*he, they*).

3. The object can be a noun (*rice, their children*) or a pronoun (*it, them*).

4. We often use a pronoun in place of a noun. Here are the subject and object pronouns.

Subject Pronouns	Object Pronouns
I	me
you	you
he	him
she	her
it	it
we	us
they	them

Practice

Replace the underlined words with a subject or object pronoun.

1. <u>John Blackie</u> is our teacher.

   He is our teacher   .

2. He uses <u>this book</u> to teach grammar.

   He uses it to teach grammar   .

3. <u>My friend and I</u> study English at the same school.

   _____.

4. He teaches <u>the students and me</u> English grammar.

   _____.

5. The students like <u>John Blackie</u>.

   _____.

6. <u>The students</u> ask John Blackie questions.

   _____.

7. He answers <u>the questions</u>.

   _____.

8. Linda is a student in our class. <u>Linda</u> always asks questions.

   _____.

9. We don't like to listen to <u>Linda</u>, but Mr. Blackie is very patient.

   _____.

10. <u>Mr. Blackie</u> always answers her questions.

   _____.

2 Practice

Complete the sentences with subject or object pronouns.

A.

At the moment, I am studying English. _____It_____ is a difficult language. Most of
                                           1
my friends are in the school with _____. Our teachers are good, but
                                      2
_____ give us a lot of homework. _____ are having a test next week. I
      3   **4**
want to pass _____. Then my parents will not worry about _____ so much.
                  5   **6**

B.

John: Do you know that woman?

Pete: Yes, I work with _____.
                                1

John: Is she nice?

Pete: Yes, _____ is very nice. We work in the same office. Come with
                    2
          _____ to the office and I will introduce you to _____. Her
                3   **4**
          husband is my boss. _____ is a great boss. Do you want me to
                                    5
          introduce you to _____ too?
                                6

John: No. That's OK.

C.

Nick: My father bought me a new computer, but I don't know how to use

          _____. Can you help _____?
                1   **2**

Dave: Sure, I'll show _____ how it works. When do you want _____
                              3   **4**
          to teach you?

Nick: Can you come tomorrow?

Dave: OK. I'll see _____ at ten tomorrow. You need to learn some basic
                            5
          steps. You can learn _____ in a few hours.
                                    6

3 | Your Turn

A.
Think of the names of your favorite people and things. You can use ideas from the list or your own.

athlete   movie star   singer
movie   restaurant   TV program

Find out from your partner why he or she likes or doesn't like them.

Example:

You: Do you like (name)?
Your partner: I like (name) because she is very...
                OR
                I don't like (name) because she is too...

B.
Write a paragraph about the person or thing that you talked about in Part A.

Example:

My favorite opera singer is...

_____

_____

_____

_____

_____

_____

_____

_____

_____

_____

_____

10b Indirect Objects

Tony gave **Karen** some flowers.

1. Some sentences have two objects after a verb: a direct object and an indirect object. A direct object answers the question *what* or *whom** (or *who*). An indirect object answers the question *to whom* or *to what*.

Subject	Verb	Direct Object	*To* + Indirect Object
I	sent	a gift	to **my mother.**

2. We can put the indirect object before the direct object. Then we do not use a preposition (*to*).

Subject	Verb	Indirect Object	Direct Object
I	sent	**my mother**	a gift.

3. When the direct object is a pronoun, we put the pronoun before the indirect object.

Subject	Verb	Pronoun Direct Object	Indirect Object
I	sent	**it**	to my mother.

4. These verbs follow the patterns above:

e-mail	hand	mail	send	tell
give	lend	pass	show	write

* In speech and informal writing, we usually use *who* for objects. In formal writing, we use *whom*.

4 Practice

Underline the direct object and circle the indirect object.

1. The teacher handed <u>the paper</u> to (me).

2. He sends newspapers to my parents.

3. She showed the photos to us.

4. My grandfather told stories to us.

5. I write letters to my brother.

6. John passed the book to Maria.

7. We lent ten dollars to Kim.

8. My father gave a watch to me.

5 Practice

Look at Practice 4. Rewrite the sentences to change the position of the indirect object. Do not use *to*.

1. *The teacher handed me the paper* .

2. _____ .

3. _____ .

4. _____ .

5. _____ .

6. _____ .

7. _____ .

8. _____ .

6 Practice

Underline the direct objects. Then change the direct objects to pronouns. Rewrite the sentences.

1. Jim: I gave my mother <u>the house</u>.

   Tom: Who did you give it to?

   Jim: *I gave it to my mother* .

2. Jim: I sold Mr. Black my car.

Tom: Who did you sell it to?

Jim: _____.

3. Jim: I offered my neighbor the television.

Tom: Who did you offer it to?

Jim: _____.

4. Jim: I sent my friends some email.

Tom: Who did you send it to?

Jim: _____.

5. Jim: I told my boss the news.

Tom: Who did you tell it to?

Jim: _____.

6. Jim: I showed my friends the photos.

Tom: Who did you show them to?

Jim: _____.

7 Your Turn

A.

It's a classmate's birthday. Say four things you can do using verbs from the list.

email   give   send   write

Example:
Let's give him a photo of the class.

B.

Now write sentences about what you can do for your classmate's birthday. Add one of your own.

1. _____.

2. _____.

3. _____.

4. _____.

5. _____.

10c Indirect Objects with *For*

Tony opened the door **for us**.

1. We use *for* with the indirect object with some verbs. With these verbs, the direct object comes first, then *for* + the indirect object.

Subject	Verb	Direct Object	Indirect Object
My father	fixed	my bicycle	**for me.**

2. These verbs take *for* + indirect object:

answer   cash   fix   open   prepare   pronounce

CORRECT: My teacher answered the questions **for me**.
INCORRECT: My teacher answered ~~me the questions~~.

Practice

Complete the sentences with *to* or *for*.

1. A teacher answers questions ____*for*____ the students.
2. A server shows the menu _____ you in a restaurant.
3. A teacher pronounces words _____ the students.
4. A comedian tells jokes _____ you.
5. A teller in a bank cashes checks _____ its customers.
6. A customer hands money _____ a salesperson.
7. A mechanic fixes cars _____ customers.
8. A teacher gives tests _____ the students.
9. A customer sends a check _____ the gas company.
10. A cook prepares food _____ customers.
11. A reader writes a letter _____ the newspaper.

9 Your Turn

What do you do for friends and family on special holidays? Make sentences with verbs from the list.

email	give	open	send	tell
fix	hand	prepare	show	write

Example:
We hand envelopes with money to our children.
We open the door for our guests.

10 Your Turn

Make a request for each situation with *Could you... , please?*

Example:
You want to open the door, but your hands are full. What do you say to your husband?
Could you open the door for me, please?

1. You have a check. You want to cash it. What do you say to the cashier?
2. Your computer does not work. Your friend can fix computers. What do you say to your friend?
3. Your hands are wet. The phone rings. What do you say to your sister?

10d Indirect Objects with Certain Verbs

She bought gifts **for me**.

1. We can use two patterns with the verbs *buy, get,* and *make*.

Verb	With *For*	Without *For*
buy	She bought gifts **for** you.	She bought you gifts.
get	I got a tie **for** my father.	I got my father a tie.
make	Jim made breakfast **for** his son.	Jim made his son breakfast.

2. We can use only one pattern with the verbs *explain, introduce,* and *repeat*.

Verb	With *To* or *For*
explain	I explained the problem **to the teacher**.
introduce	He introduced me **to the teacher**.
repeat	The teacher repeated the rules **for us**.

CORRECT: She explained the answer to me.
INCORRECT: She explained ~~me the answer.~~

11 Practice

Jenny is preparing gifts. Complete the sentences with the words in parentheses. Write each sentence two ways as in the example.

1. She bought (a tie/her father) _She bought a tie for her father. She_
   bought him a tie.

2. She got (a blouse/her mother) _____

_____

3. She made (a sweater/her brother) _____

_____

4. She bought (a toy/her niece) _____

_____

5. She got (books/her sister) _____

_____

6. She made (a cake/her neighbors) _____

_____

7. She bought (a wallet/Brian) _____

_____

8. She got (a plant/her boss) _____

_____

9. She made (cookies/her roommate) _____

_____

12 Practice

Complete the sentences with the words in parentheses.

1. The teacher explained (us/the answer)

   The teacher explained the answer to us .

2. The teacher introduced (us/indirect objects)

   _____ .

3. The teacher repeated (us/the questions)

   _____ .

4. The teacher explained (me/the meaning of the word)

   _____ .

5. The student repeated (her/the sentence)

_____.

6. The teacher introduced (us/the new student)

_____.

7. The student explained (the teacher/her problem)

_____.

8. The teacher introduced (the class/the speaker)

_____.

9. The teacher repeated (us/the difficult words)

_____.

| 13 | Practice |

Make sentences with the words in parentheses. Use _to_ or _for_ where necessary. In some cases, two patterns are possible.

1. Tim bought (his wife/a gift)

Tim bought a gift for his wife _____.

2. He fixed (her/the car)

_____.

3. He made (dinner/her)

_____.

4. He got (flowers/her)

_____.

5. He opened (the door/her)

_____.

6. He showed (a letter/her)

_____.

7. He explained (his problem/her)

_____.

8. His wife told (her ideas/him)

_____.

9. She gave (advice/him)

_____.

14

Your Turn

What are you going to do next month? Use the verbs from the list to make sentences.

buy	get	open	show
fix	make	prepare	tell

Example:
I am going to buy a present for my wife. It's her birthday.

10e Possessive Pronouns

John: Is this pen **yours**?

Ken: No, it's not **mine**.

I think it's Susan's.

Possessive Pronoun	Possessive Adjective
mine	my
yours	your
hers	her
his	his
its	its
ours	our
yours	your
theirs	their

1. We put a possessive adjective before a noun. A possessive pronoun is used alone.

   This is **my** pen. This pen is **mine**.
   That is **their** television. It's **theirs**.

2. We use possessive pronouns and possessive adjectives to show that something belongs to somebody.

   Excuse me, is this **your** umbrella? OR Excuse me, is this **yours**?

3. Do not confuse *its* and *it's*.

   Its is a possessive adjective.

   The bus needs **its** tire fixed.

   It's is a contraction of *it is*.

   It's time to go.

15 Practice

Match the objects with the people. Write sentences using the possessive forms as in the example.

nurse

teacher

taxi driver

travelers

children

books

1. _These are the teacher's books_ .
   These are her books .
   These are hers .

thermometer

2. _____ .
_____ .
_____ .

suitcases

3. _____ .
_____ .
_____ .

taxi

4. _____ .
_____ .
_____ .

toys

5. _____ .
_____ .
_____ .

16 Practice

Look at Practice 15 and answer the questions.

1. Are the books the teacher's?

_Yes, they're hers_____.

2. Is the thermometer the taxi driver's?

_No, it's not his_____.

3. Are the suitcases the travelers'?

_____.

4. Is the taxi the teacher's?

_____.

5. Are the toys the nurse's?

_____.

6. Are the toys the children's?

_____.

17 Practice

Circle the correct form.

1. Karen: Don't forget ((your)/ yours) umbrella!

Jamie: That's not my umbrella. (My / Mine) is black.

2. Jim: Do the Petersons live here?

Dave: Yes, they do.

Jim: Is that (their / theirs) house?

Dave: No, it isn't. (Theirs / Their) is around the corner.

3. Bobby: That's (my / mine) teddy bear!

Jenny: No, it isn't! It's (mine / my) teddy bear.

Mother: Stop it children! Jenny, give Bobby his teddy bear.

Jenny: It isn't his. It's (mine / my).

4. My brother rents his apartment, and I rent (my / mine) apartment.

His apartment is small, but (my / mine) is big.

5. Tony: Where is (their / theirs) car parked?

    Pete: (Their / Theirs) is on the street.

    Tony: Is Maria's car on the street too?

    Pete: No, (her / hers) is in the driveway.

6. Ben: Shall we take (your / yours) car or (my / mine) car?

    Jerry: Let's take (my / mine). It's faster than (your / yours).

    Ben: Yes, but (my/mine) car is more comfortable.

7. Suzy: Is that (your / yours) bag over there?

    Laura: No, it isn't (my / mine). I thought it was (your / yours).

8. (Our / Ours) classroom is very nice and bright. The teacher has (her / hers) table and

chair, and we have (our / ours).

18   Practice

Complete the sentences with *it's* and *its*.

1. <u>It's</u> cold outside so take a coat.

2. My sofa was old, so I changed _____ cover.

3. _____ not far. You can walk.

4. The store is near here, but I can't remember _____ name.

5. _____ a beautiful apartment. How much is the rent?

6. How much is the jacket? I don't see _____ price.

7. A: Who is it?

    B: _____ me.

8. The new town has _____ bank and shopping area in the center.

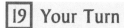

19 **Your Turn**

Work with a partner. Compare your hair, eyes, shoes, hands, etc.

Example:
My hair is long. Yours is short.

10f Indefinite Pronouns

Form

Ken: Excuse me, there's **something** in my soup.
Server: I don't see **anything**, sir.

	Some-	*Any-*	*No-*
Things	something	anything	nothing
People	someone	anyone	no one

Function

1. We use *some-* (*something, someone*), and *no-* (*nothing, no one*) in affirmative statements.

   Someone is at the door.

2. We use *any-* (*anything, anyone*) in negative statements.

   I can't see **anyone**.

3. We use *some-* or *any-* in questions.

   Can you see **something**? OR Can you see **anything**?

20 Practice

Complete the sentences with *something, someone, anything, anyone, nothing,* **and** *no one.*

1. Lin: There's _____ *someone* _____ at the door.

   Jim: There's _____ *no one* _____ here. There must be _____ *something* _____

   wrong with your ears!

2. John: Let's have _____ to eat. How about a sandwich?

   Pete: No, thanks. I'm not hungry. I don't want _____ to eat.

3. I went to the store to buy _____ for Jamie's birthday. But there

   was _____! So I didn't buy _____.

4. Kim: Is there _____ in the mail for me?

   Nancy: Sorry, there's _____ for you, but there's

   _____ for me.

5. Sylvia: I think there's _____ in my eye.

   Ben: Your eye is red, but I can't see _____ in it.

6. _____ is wrong. Jim is never late. Does _____

   know _____?

7. Don: Did you lose _____?

   Kevin: No, I didn't lose _____. I just can't see

   _____ without my glasses.

8. Mike: Do you know _____ about Japanese history?

   Bob: _____, sorry. Maybe Tony knows _____.

   Ask him.

9. Kim: I'm thirsty. Is there _____ in the fridge?

Lena: No, there's _____. How about _____ hot, like tea?

10. Erik: Do you hear _____?

Louis: No, I don't hear _____.

Erik: Do you see _____?

Louis: No, I don't see _____.

21 Your Turn

Think of a person. The class asks questions with *anyone*. You answer in complete sentences with *someone* or *anyone*.

Example:

Class: Is he/she anyone in this class?

You: Yes, he/she is someone in this class.

Class: Is he/she anyone with black hair?

You: No, he/she isn't anyone with black hair.

Write a paragraph about gifts.

Step 1.   Work with a partner. Ask questions like these about a person your partner sends cards and gifts to. Write the answers to the questions.

1.   Who is a person you always send a card or give a gift to?
2.   On what occasion (birthday, Valentine's Day, Christmas, etc.) do you send a card?
3.   What kind of card do you usually send this person? (funny card, card with flowers, etc.) What do you say in the card?
4.   What kind of gifts do you get for this person? How much money or time do you spend on a gift? Do you like to buy gifts for this person, or is it difficult to buy a gift?
5.   Does this person also send you a card and buy you gifts?
6.   Do you like your cards and gifts? Do you keep them?

Step 2.   Rewrite your answers in paragraph form. For more writing guidelines, see pages 190-195.

Step 3.   Write a title in three or four words, for example, "Cards and Gifts."

Step 4.   Evaluate your paragraph.

Checklist

_____   Did you indent the first line?
_____   Did you give your paragraph a title?
_____   Did you use capital letters correctly?
_____   Did you use verb tenses correctly?

Step 5.   Work with your partner to edit your paragraph. Correct spelling, punctuation, vocabulary, and grammar.

Step 6.   Write your final copy.

SELF-TEST

A **Choose the best answer, A, B, C, or D, to complete the sentence. Mark your answer by darkening the oval with the same letter.**

1. Mr. Cotton sold _____.

    A. Tim it   Ⓐ Ⓑ Ⓒ Ⓓ
    B. to Tim it
    C. for Tim it
    D. it to Tim

2. Ken introduced _____.

    A. me his friend   Ⓐ Ⓑ Ⓒ Ⓓ
    B. me to his friend
    C. his friend me
    D. for me his friend

3. The teacher explained _____.

    A. me the question   Ⓐ Ⓑ Ⓒ Ⓓ
    B. for me the question
    C. the question to me
    D. the question me

4. We sent _____.

    A. to Jim a letter   Ⓐ Ⓑ Ⓒ Ⓓ
    B. for Jim a letter
    C. a letter Jim
    D. a letter to Jim

5. I didn't _____ yesterday. I just watched television.

    A. do anything   Ⓐ Ⓑ Ⓒ Ⓓ
    B. do nothing
    C. do something
    D. anything do

6. John gave _____.

    A. the check me   Ⓐ Ⓑ Ⓒ Ⓓ
    B. for me the check
    C. to me the check
    D. me the check

7. Could you please _____?

    A. lend to me it   Ⓐ Ⓑ Ⓒ Ⓓ
    B. lend for me it
    C. lend me it
    D. lend it to me

8. The students handed _____.

    A. their papers to   Ⓐ Ⓑ Ⓒ Ⓓ
        the teacher
    B. their papers
        the teacher
    C. to the teacher their papers
    D. for the teacher their papers

9. My friend fixed _____.

    A. for me my car   Ⓐ Ⓑ Ⓒ Ⓓ
    B. my car to me
    C. my car for me
    D. to me my car

10. We prepared _____.

    A. dinner to our friends   Ⓐ Ⓑ Ⓒ Ⓓ
    B. dinner for our friends
    C. our friends dinner
    D. dinner for ours friends

B Find the underlined word or phrase, A, B, C, or D, that is incorrect. Mark your answer by darkening the oval with the same letter.

1. Most people send birthday cards for their
    A B C

   friends and relatives.
    D

   Ⓐ Ⓑ Ⓒ Ⓓ

2. The Chinese have theirs New Year in
    A B C

   January or February.
    D

   Ⓐ Ⓑ Ⓒ Ⓓ

3. In Antarctica, there isn't something for
    A B C

   the penguins to make their nests with.
    D

   Ⓐ Ⓑ Ⓒ Ⓓ

4. Doctors tell ours what to do when we
    A B C

   get sick.
    D

   Ⓐ Ⓑ Ⓒ Ⓓ

5. Do you know anyone about Mexican
    A B C

   customs?
    D

   Ⓐ Ⓑ Ⓒ Ⓓ

6. Plants make theirs food from simple
    A B

   things like air and water.
    C D

   Ⓐ Ⓑ Ⓒ Ⓓ

7. A baby chimpanzee will travel some of the
    A

   time on it mother's back until it is about
    B C

   five years old.
    D

   Ⓐ Ⓑ Ⓒ Ⓓ

8. The brain needs a lot of energy to do it
    A B C D

   work.

   Ⓐ Ⓑ Ⓒ Ⓓ

9. Could you please explain me the reason?
    A B C D

   Ⓐ Ⓑ Ⓒ Ⓓ

10. Most supermarkets give theirs customers
     A B

    free grocery bags for their purchases.
     C D

    Ⓐ Ⓑ Ⓒ Ⓓ

UNIT 11

MODALS

11a *Can*

Bears **can climb** trees.
Bears **can't fly.**

AFFIRMATIVE AND NEGATIVE STATEMENTS			
Subject	*Can*	Base Verb	
I		**ski.**	
You		**swim.**	
	can	**speak**	French.
He/She/It	**cannot**	**cook**	rice.
	can't	**drive**	a car.
We		**climb**	trees.
They		**sleep.**	

Function

We use *can* to talk about ability in the present.

I come from Italy. I **can speak** Italian, but I **can't speak** Japanese.
Yuko comes from Japan. She **can't speak** Italian, but she **can speak** Japanese.
Ted **can play** the piano, but he **can't play** the guitar.

☐ Practice

A.

What do you know about animals? Look at the chart and write affirmative sentences and negative sentences about the animals.

Animal		Verb
Elephants		fly.
Birds		swim.
Chickens		make honey.
Bees	can/can't	climb trees.
Horses		sing.
Penguins		run.
Monkeys		see at night.
Dogs		lie down.

Affirmative Sentences

1. *Elephants can swim*   .
2. _____ .
3. _____ .
4. _____ .
5. _____ .
6. _____ .
7. _____ .
8. _____ .

Negative Sentences

1. *Elephants can't fly*   .
2. _____ .
3. _____ .
4. _____ .
5. _____ .
6. _____ .
7. _____ .
8. _____ .

B.
Discuss these questions with a partner.

1. What are some animals and the special things they do?
Example:
Whales can stay under water for a long time.

2. What can humans do that animals can't?
Example:
You: Humans can build things. Animals can't.
Your partner: Well, some animals can build things. For example, birds can make nests.

2 Your Turn

Make sentences about yourself with *I can* or *I can't*.

Example:
write with my left hand
You: I can write with my left hand.   OR   I can't write with my left hand.

1. write with both hands

   *I can't write with both hands*_____.

2. eat with chopsticks

   _____.

3. see without glasses

   _____.

4. drink tea without sugar

   _____.

5. stand on my head

   _____.

6. type fast

   _____.

7. cook pasta

   _____.

8. ride a bicycle

   _____.

9. run three miles

   _____.

10. play basketball

    _____.

11. sing

    _____.

12. dance

    _____.

13. paint pictures

    _____.

14. sew on a button

    _____.

11b Questions with *Can*

YES/NO QUESTIONS			ANSWERS
Can	Subject	Base Verb	
	you	**speak** English?	Yes, I/we **can**.
	he	**dance** the tango?	No, he **can't**.
Can	we	**go** outside?	Yes, you **can**.
	they	**see** us?	No, they **can't**.

WH- WORD QUESTIONS				
Wh- Word	*Can*	Subject	Base Verb	
Where		I	**buy**	this book?
When	**can**	you	**come?**	
What		she	**do?**	

3 Practice

A.

Read this advertisement.

> **DAY CARE PROVIDER needed for 2 children 4 and 7 years old.**
> Requirements: Drive, cook meals, tell stories, read music, swim, draw, and have a lot of energy. Excellent pay. Please call Monica 743-8995.

B.

Monica is talking to a job applicant. Complete her questions with *can* or other question forms.

1. _____*How*_____ old _____*are*_____ you?

2. _____ drive?

3. _____ meals?

4. _____ music?

5. _____ swim?

6. _____ draw?

7. _____ stories?

8. _____ a lot of energy?

9. What other things _____ do?

10. When _____ come?

C.

Now write your answers to Monica's questions.

1. *I am 18 years old* _____.

2. _____.

3. _____.

4. _____.

5. _____.

6. _____.

7. _____.

8. _____.

9. _____.

10. _____.

4 Practice

A.

Work with a partner. Ask questions and give short answers.

Example:

use a computer

You: Can you use a computer?

Your partner: Yes, I can.   OR   No, I can't.

1. use a computer

2. ski

3. play a musical instrument

4. ride a horse/a bicycle/a motorcycle

5. drive a car

6. play chess

7. cook

8. draw or paint

9. what kind of food/cook

10. what sports/play

11. how many languages/speak

12. what/do/well

B.

Now tell the class what you and your partner *can* and *can't do*.

Example:

I can ride a bicycle, speak three languages, and cook eggs and rice.

I can't ski or play chess.

My partner can use a computer.

11c *Could*: Past of *Can*

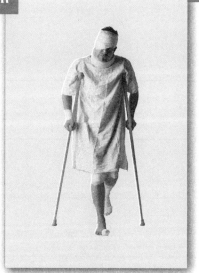

After the accident last week, he **couldn't see**, and **he couldn't run**.
He **could talk.**

	AFFIRMATIVE AND NEGATIVE STATEMENTS		
Subject	*Could (Not)*	Base Verb	
I		**come**	to class yesterday.
You	**could**	**do**	the homework.
He/She	**couldn't**	**find**	the store.
We	**could not**	**go**	to the concert.
They			

	YES/NO QUESTIONS			SHORT ANSWERS
	I	**run**	fast?	Yes, you **could.**
	you	**ride**	a bicycle?	Yes, I/we **could.**
Could	she/he	**finish**	the test?	No, she/he **couldn't.**
	we	**eat**	the food?	No, you/the **couldn't.**
	they	**play**	tennis?	Yes, they **could.**

Function

Could is the past form of can. We use *could* or *could not (couldn't)* for ability in the past.

I **could ride** a bicycle when I was five.
I **couldn't read.**
Could you **read** when you were six?

5 Practice

Mary is twenty-five years old now. What can she do now that she couldn't do when she was two years old? Write sentences with the words and phrases below.

A.

1. ride a bicycle

She couldn't ride a bicycle   .

2. run fast

_____ .

3. drive a car

_____ .

4. ski

_____ .

5. take tests

_____ .

6. work

_____ .

7. dance

_____ .

B.
Write three things you couldn't do before that you can do now.

1. *Five years ago, I couldn't swim, but I can swim well now*   .

2. _____ .

3. _____ .

6 Practice

Andy was at home last month with a broken leg. What could he do? What couldn't he do? Write sentences about Andy using words from the list.

drive	play tennis	swim	watch TV
go to school	read magazines	visit friends	work online

1. *He couldn't go to school*   .

2. _____ .

3. _____ .

4. _____ .

5. _____ .

6. _____ .

7. _____ .

8. _____ .

7 Practice

Work with a partner. Ask what your partner could do when he or she was six years old.

Example:
play the piano
You: Could you play the piano?
Your partner: Yes, I could.   OR   No, I couldn't.

1. read
2. swim
3. paint pictures
4. write
5. use a computer
6. use the telephone
7. count to a hundred
8. ride a bicycle

9. tell the time
10. take photographs
11. sing
12. ride a horse
13. climb trees
14. make a sandwich
15. brush your teeth
16. eat with chopsticks

11d *Be Able To*

Hercules Lewis is very strong. He **is able to** lift three people at the same time.

PRESENT				PAST			
Subject	Form of *Be*	*Able To*	Base Verb	Subject	Form of *Be*	*Able To*	Base Verb
I	**am**			I	**was**		
You	**are**			You	**were**		
He She It	**is**	**able to**	go.	He She It	**was**	**able to**	go.
We They	**are**			We They	**were**		

FUTURE			
Subject	Form of *Be*	*Able To*	Base Verb
I			
You			
He She It We They	**will be**	**able to**	go.

86

Unit II

We can use *be able to* in place of *can* or *could* for ability in the present, future, and past.

Past
He **wasn't able to finish** the test yesterday.   OR   He **couldn't finish** the test yesterday.

Present
She **is able to run** five miles.   OR   She **can run** five miles.*

Future
I'**ll be able to go** out tomorrow.   OR   I **can go** out tomorrow.

* *Can* is more common than *be able to* in the present tense.

8 Read

Read about Mozart. Change the underlined forms of *can/could* to forms of *be able to*.

Mozart was born in Austria in 1756. His father was a musician. At age three, he <u>could play</u> the piano. After he heard a piece of music one time, Mozart <u>could play</u> it.
1   **2**
People <u>couldn't believe</u> their ears! At age five, he <u>could write</u> music for the piano.
3   **4**
Soon his father <u>couldn't teach</u> him because little Mozart knew everything. At twelve,
5
he was famous and <u>could make</u> money for his family.
6

Mozart worked long hours and <u>could work</u> very fast. He <u>could write</u> an opera in
7   **8**
just a few weeks. He <u>could work</u> better at night because it was quiet. He <u>could write</u>
9   **10**
all kinds of music, even music for clocks. In all, he wrote over 600 pieces of music.

Mozart died at age 35. We still <u>cannot understand</u> why he died. Today, we still
11
listen to Mozart at concerts. We <u>can buy</u> his music on tapes or CDs. Believe it or
12
not, Mozart is still the world's best-selling composer!

1. _was able to play_

2. _____

3. _____

4. _____

5. _____

6. _____

7. _____

8. _____

9. _____

10. _____

11. _____

12. _____

A.

This is Tommy. He is nine years old now.
Complete the sentences to say what he can do
now, what he could do when he was a baby and
what he will be able to do when he is 16.

Baby	Now (age 9)	Age 16
smile	use a computer	dance
sleep	ride a bicycle	drive a car
cry	play football	sing in a group
eat	run	get a part-time job

1. When he was a baby, *he could smile* _____.

2. Now, *he can use a computer* _____.

3. When he is 16, *he will be able to dance* _____.

4. When he was a baby, _____.

5. Now, _____.

6. When he is 16, _____.

7. When he was a baby, _____.

8. Now, _____.

9. When he is 16, _____.

10. When he was a baby, _____.

11. Now, _____.

12. When he is 16, _____.

B.
Say three things you will be able to do in the future.

Example:
I will be able to talk to people on the telephone in English.

11e *Should*

In China and Japan you **should bow** when you greet someone.

AFFIRMATIVE AND NEGATIVE STATEMENTS

Subject	*Should*	Base Verb
I		
You	**should**	
He/She/It	**should not**	**go.**
We	**shouldn't**	
They		

YES/NO QUESTIONS			SHORT ANSWERS
Should	Subject	Base Verb	
Should	I		Yes, you **should.**
	you		No, I/we **shouldn't.**
	he/she/it	**go?**	Yes, she **should.**
	we		No, you **shouldn't.**
	they		Yes, they **should.**

Function

1. We use *should* to give advice. *Should* means it's a good idea to do something.

   Dick is very sick. He **should see** a doctor.
   Nancy is still working at 3:00 in the morning. She **should go** to bed.

2. We use *shouldn't (should not)* when it's a bad idea to do something.

   You **shouldn't drive** in the storm. It's dangerous.
   Jimmy **shouldn't eat** the whole cake. He'll get sick.

10 Practice

Jim is going to Asia. Give him advice. Complete the sentences with *should* or *shouldn't*.

1. You ___shouldn't___ speak fast. Your audience may not understand you.

2. If you don't know what to do, you _____ ask someone.

3. You _____ blow your nose in front of other people at a meeting.

4. You _____ be on time for class.

5. You _____ greet older people first.

6. You _____ use your hands too much when you speak. A hand sign may have a different meaning there.

11 Practice

Nick is a teenager. Tell what Nick should or shouldn't do.

1. He skips school.

   _He shouldn't skip school_____.

2. He comes home late.

   _____.

3. He doesn't do his homework.

   _____.

4. He doesn't listen to his parents.

   _____.

5. He doesn't listen in class.

_____.

6. He doesn't clean up his room.

_____.

7. He asks his parents for money every day.

_____.

8. He's not nice to his brother and sister.

_____.

9. He doesn't help with the housework.

_____.

12 Practice

Give advice in these situations.

1. Ted has a very bad cold and he is at work.

_He should go to bed_____

_____.

2. Alex has a test tomorrow, but he hasn't studied for it. He wants to watch television right now.

_____

_____.

3. Tim often goes to bed late and gets up late. He's often late for work.

_____

_____.

4. When it's cold outside, Joe wears a T-shirt.

_____

_____.

5. The coffee in the restaurant is cold. You cannot see the waiter.

_____

_____.

6. Ken is making a salad. He has not washed his hands, and he hasn't washed the vegetables for the salad.

_____

_____.

7. Ken is overweight and has health problems because of his weight. He drives everywhere. He even drives to the corner store to get his cigarettes.

_____

_____.

11f *Must*

You **mustn't talk** in class.

AFFIRMATIVE AND NEGATIVE STATEMENTS			
Subject	*Must (Not)*	Base Verb	
I			
You	**must**		
He/She/It	**must not**	**talk**	in class.
We	**mustn't**		
They			

Note: Questions with *must* are formal and not very common. They are formed like questions with *can* and *should*.

What **must** I do?

1. We use *must* to say that something is very important or necessary. We often use *must* for rules or strong advice. We use *must not (mustn't)* when something is against the law or rules or isn't right.

> I **must go** to the bank. I have no more money. (It's a necessity; there is no other choice.)
> You **mustn't park** here. (It is against the law or rules.)

2. *Must* is stronger than *should*. When we use *must*, we have no choice. When we use *should*, we have a choice.

> I **should go** to the bank. (It's a good idea, but not necessary.)
> You **shouldn't park** here. (It's not a good idea, but you can if you want.)

13 Practice

Complete the following class rules with *must* or *mustn't*.

1. _You must_____ be quiet when someone else is speaking.

2. _____ listen to the teacher.

3. _____ arrive in class on time.

4. _____ eat in class.

5. _____ use a telephone in class.

6. _____ answer the teacher's questions.

7. _____ go to sleep.

8. _____ attend class every day.

9. _____ bring your books to class.

10. _____ do homework.

11. _____ cheat or copy in a test.

12. _____ write letters to friends in class.

14 Practice

Hotel Iron Sides is the only hotel in a small town. The hotel has many strict rules. Change the rules to sentences with *must* or *mustn't*.

Hotel Rules

Do not smoke in your room.

Do not take food into your room.

Pay for your room on the day you arrive.

No credit cards or checks are accepted.

Do not wash clothes in your room.

Do not bring visitors to your room.

Return to the hotel by 10:00 P.M. every night.

Turn off the television after 10:00 P.M.

Leave your key at the reception desk when you go out.

Ask the reception desk if you want to use the telephone.

Leave your room by 9:00 A.M. on the day you leave.

1. _You mustn't_ smoke in your room.

2. _____ take food into your room.

3. _____ pay for your room on the day you arrive.

4. _____ pay with cash.

5. _____ wash clothes in your room.

6. _____ bring visitors to your room.

7. _____ return by 10:00 P.M. every night.

8. _____ turn off the television after 10:00 P.M. at night.

9. _____ leave your key at the reception desk when you go out.

10. _____ ask the reception desk if you want to use the telephone.

11. _____ leave your room by 9:00 A.M. on the day you leave.

15

Practice

Work with a partner. Write sentences using *must* and *mustn't* for the following situations.

1. when you are in a library

   When you are in a library, you must be quiet   .

   When you are in a library, you mustn't eat   .

2. when you are on an airplane

   _____ .

   _____ .

3. before you leave the country

   _____ .

   _____ .

4. when you take a test

   _____ .

   _____ .

5. when you drive

   _____ .

   _____ .

6. when you eat at a restaurant

   _____ .

   _____ .

7. when you are shopping online

   _____ .

   _____ .

8. when you are at a concert

   _____ .

   _____ .

11g *Have To*

Bill

Ken

Bill **has to get up** at 5:00 A.M. to work in the garden.

Ken **doesn't have to get** up at 5:00 A.M.

But he **has to wear** a suit to work.

PRESENT

AFFIRMATIVE STATEMENTS			NEGATIVE STATEMENTS			
Subject	*Have To*	Base Verb	Subject	*Do/Does Not*	*Have To*	Base Verb
I	**have to**		I	**do not**		
You			You	**don't**		
He	**has to**	**work.**	He	**does not**	**have to**	**work.**
She			She			
It			It	**doesn't**		
We	**have to**		We	**do not**		
They			They	**don't**		

YES/NO QUESTIONS				SHORT ANSWERS
Do/Does	Subject	*Have To*	Base Verb	
Do	I	**have to**	**work?**	Yes, you **do.**
	you			No, I/we **don't.**
Does	he/she/it			Yes, he/she/it **does.**
Do	we			Yes, you **do.**
	they			No, they **don't.**

96

Unit II

PAST

AFFIRMATIVE STATEMENTS			NEGATIVE STATEMENTS			
Subject	*Had to*	Base Verb	Subject	*Did Not*	*Have To*	Base Verb
I			I			
You			You			
He			He			
She	**had to**	**work.**	She	**did not**	**have to**	**work.**
It			It	**didn't**		
We			We			
They			They			

YES/NO QUESTIONS				SHORT ANSWERS
Did	Subject	*Have To*	Base Verb	
	I			Yes, you **did.**
	you			No, I/we **didn't.**
Did	he/she/it	**have to**	**work?**	No, he/she/it **didn't.**
	we			Yes, you **did.**
	they			No, they **didn't.**

Function

1. We use *have to* for something that is necessary. But *have to* is not as strong as *must*. *Have to* means the same as *need to*:

   We **have to study** for the test.
   OR   We **need to study** for the test.

   Joe **has to wear** a suit for his new job.
   OR   Joe **needs to wear** a suit for his new job.

2. We use *don't have to* and *didn't have to* for the negative. *Don't/doesn't/didn't have to* means that something is not or was not necessary. There is a choice.

   Tomorrow is Saturday. We **don't have to study** tonight.
   Tim **didn't have to wait** at the airport yesterday.

3. We use *do/does...have to...?* and *did...have to..?* to ask if something is necessary.

   Do we **have to go** to school tomorrow?   Yes, you **do.**
   Did you **have to work** late yesterday?   No, I **didn't.**

16 Practice

What do you have to do in your English class? Make sentences with *have to* or *don't have to*.

1. _We have to_ learn grammar rules.

2. _____ write compositions.

3. _____ learn vocabulary.

4. _____ answer questions in English.

5. _____ read newspapers.

6. _____ sing songs.

7. _____ take tests.

8. _____ complete exercises.

9. _____ give speeches in English.

10. _____ dance.

17 Practice

Work with a partner. Ask and answer questions about the chart. Write your answers.

Qualities	TV Journalist	Fashion Model	Doctor
have a degree			X
be a good speaker	X		
be attractive		X	
be scientific			X

1. TV journalist/have a degree

   _Does a TV journalist have to have a degree_____?

   _No, he/she doesn't_____.

2. TV journalist/be a good speaker

   _____?

   _____.

3. TV journalist/be attractive

_____?

_____.

4. TV journalist/be scientific

_____?

_____.

5. model/have a degree

_____?

_____.

6. model/be a good speaker

_____?

_____.

7. model/be attractive

_____?

_____.

8. model/be scientific

_____?

_____.

9. doctor/have a degree

_____?

_____.

10. doctor/be a good speaker

_____?

_____.

11. doctor/be attractive

_____?

_____.

12. doctor/be scientific

_____?

_____.

18 Practice

Complete the sentences with *mustn't* or *don't have to*.

1. You _don't have to_ wash it by hand. You can wash it in a washing machine.

2. You _____ park here between 9:00 A.M. and 12:00 P.M. That is when the city cleans the street.

3. You _____ buy tickets at the box office. You can buy them online.

4. You _____ smoke in this restaurant. It is against the law.

5. You _____ turn onto this street. Traffic is going one-way in the opposite direction.

6. You _____ pay for children under the age of five. They get in free.

7. You _____ rollerblade on the sidewalk. It is against park regulations.

8. You _____ pay with cash. You can use a credit card.

19 Practice

A.
**This is Gloria Glamour. She was a famous movie star. She was also a millionaire.
Complete the sentences with *had to* or *didn't have to*.**

1. She _____ had to _____ wear make up.

2. She _____ drive her car. She had a chauffeur.

3. She _____ wait for the bus.

4. She _____ meet important people.

5. She _____ clean her house. She paid someone to clean

her house for her.

6. She _____ act in movies.

7. She _____ sing and dance.

8. She _____ look beautiful.

B.
What other things did she have to or not have to do? Make sentences with a partner.

---

20 Your Turn

A.
1. Tell your partner three things you had to do as a child.
2. Tell your partner three things you didn't have to do as a child.

Examples:
I had to go to bed at 8:00 P.M.
I didn't have to cook dinner.

B.
Write sentences about what your partner had to do and didn't have to do as a child.

Example:
Suzanne had to clean her room, but she didn't have to wash dishes.

1. _____ .

2. _____ .

3. _____ .

4. _____ .

5. _____ .

6. _____ .

11h *May I, Can I,* and *Could I*

Form

Teller: **May I** see your driver's license or a piece of identification?

Woman: **Yes, of course.** Here it is.

Teller: Thanks.

QUESTIONS				SHORT ANSWERS	
May/Can Could	*I*	Base Verb		Affirmative	Negative
May **Can** **Could**	**I**	**see**	your license?	Of course. Certainly. Sure.* OK.* No problem.*	I'm sorry, no.
May **Can** **Could**	**I**	**help**	you?	Yes, please.	No, thanks.

* Use these expressions with friends or family members.

Function

Hotel Desk: **May I** help you?

Guest: **Could I** have the key to Room 17 please?

1. We use *may I, can I,* and *could I* to ask for permission. We also use these expressions to offer to help someone else.

2. *May I, can I,* and *could I* have the same meaning, but *may I* is the most polite or formal. *Could I* is more polite than *can I. Could I* is appropriate in almost all situations.

21 Practice

Complete the dialogues with *may I, can I*, or *could I*.

1. Student: <u>May I</u> go home early?

   Teacher: No, you may not.

2. Student: _____ borrow your dictionary?

   Classmate: Sure.

3. Brother: _____ use your phone?

   Sister: No, you can't.

4. Customer: _____ have another glass of water?

   Waiter: Certainly, sir.

5. Employee: _____ ask a question, sir?

   Director of company: Yes, of course.

6. Police Officer: _____ see your driver's license?

   Driver: Yes. Here it is.

22 Practice

Work with a partner. Ask and answer questions with *may I, can I*, and *could I* in these situations.

Example:
You are a teenager. You want to go to a party tonight. Ask a parent.

Teenager: Can I go to a party tonight please, Dad?
Father: OK, you can go, but be back at 11:00.

1. You're an attendant at the theater. You want to see a person's ticket.

2. You are a customer in a restaurant. You do not have a fork to eat with. Ask the server.

3. You work in an office. You want to speak to your boss for a moment. Ask your boss.

4. Your teacher is carrying a lot of books. Ask if you can help.

5. Your friend is having trouble with her computer. You can fix it. Ask her.

6. You want to take next Monday off from school to go to the doctor. Ask your teacher.

7. You want to watch a movie on television tonight at 9:00. There is only one television in the house. Your sister is the only person who watches it. Ask your sister.

8. You are in a cafeteria with a tray of food. There is only one empty seat at a table, but there is someone sitting at the table. Ask if you can sit there.

WRITING: Write a Letter of Advice

Write a letter offering advice.

Step 1. Read the situation and tell what your friend *should/shouldn't* do, *must/must not* do, and *has/doesn't have to* do.

A friend is coming to your country. The friend is invited to dinner at an important person's house and has asked for your advice.

1. take flowers/gift
2. wear nice/clean clothes
3. take shoes/coat off
4. be late/early arriving
5. bring a friend
6. say the food is good/bad

Step 2. Write the six sentences from Step 1. Add your own ideas.

1. *You should take a gift* .   4. _____ .
2. _____ .   5. _____ .
3. _____ .   6. _____ .

Step 3. Rewrite your sentences as the second paragraph in the letter below. For more writing guidelines, see pages 190-195.

```
                                              May 1, 20XX

    Dear Anita,
        I'm so happy that you are coming for a visit. Of course,
    you will stay with us. It's exciting that you are going to have
    dinner with the mayor of our city. Here's my advice about
    that...
```

Step 4. Evaluate your paragraph.

Checklist

_____ Did you use verb tenses correctly?
_____ Did you give all of the important information that your friend will need?
_____ Did you use the words *should, must,* and *have to*?

Step 5. Edit your paragraph with a partner. Correct spelling, punctuation, vocabulary, and grammar.

Step 6. Write your final copy.

SELF-TEST

A **Choose the best answer, A, B, C, or D, to complete the sentence. Mark your answer by darkening the oval with the same letter.**

1. When you were two years old, you
   _____ ride a bicycle.

   A. couldn't   Ⓐ Ⓑ Ⓒ Ⓓ
   B. can't
   C. must not
   D. have to

2. _____ answer the door, please?

   A. May you   Ⓐ Ⓑ Ⓒ Ⓓ
   B. Could you
   C. Have I
   D. You could

3. _____ to go there?

   A. Have we to   Ⓐ Ⓑ Ⓒ Ⓓ
   B. Had we
   C. Do we
   D. Do we have

4. He _____ to his parents.

   A. should listens   Ⓐ Ⓑ Ⓒ Ⓓ
   B. should listen
   C. have to listens
   D. must to listen

5. You _____ eat in class. Eat outside!

   A. haven't to   Ⓐ Ⓑ Ⓒ Ⓓ
   B. must not to
   C. mustn't
   D. don't have

6. You _____ ask for directions. I know
   how to get there.

   A. don't have to   Ⓐ Ⓑ Ⓒ Ⓓ
   B. must not
   C. should to
   D. do not have

7. Kathy _____ speak Japanese.

   A. is able   Ⓐ Ⓑ Ⓒ Ⓓ
   B. able to
   C. is able to
   D. can able to

8. I _____ to study tonight. There's no
   school tomorrow.

   A. haven't   Ⓐ Ⓑ Ⓒ Ⓓ
   B. don't have
   C. don't has
   D. must not

9. You _____ lose this key. This is the
   only one.

   A. haven't to   Ⓐ Ⓑ Ⓒ Ⓓ
   B. shouldn't
   C. don't have to
   D. must not

10. I _____ study hard for my test
    yesterday.

    A. have to   Ⓐ Ⓑ Ⓒ Ⓓ
    B. had to
    C. must to
    D. should

B Find the underlined word or phrase, A, B, C, or D, that is incorrect. Mark your answer by darkening the oval with the same letter.

1. We <u>able to</u> <u>go</u> <u>for</u> a vacation on the moon
       A   B   C

    <u>in the future</u>.
       D

    (A) (B) (C) (D)

2. You <u>must to</u> <u>use</u> a black <u>or</u> blue pen for
        A   B   C

    the test. You cannot <u>use</u> a pencil.
                          D

    (A) (B) (C) (D)

3. A camel <u>is able</u> live without <u>any</u> <u>water</u> for
             A   B   C

    about <u>five days</u>.
           D

    (A) (B) (C) (D)

4. You must <u>have to</u> <u>a passport</u> to travel to
              A   B

    <u>another</u> <u>country</u>.
       C   D

    (A) (B) (C) (D)

5. The ostrich is <u>not able</u> to fly, <u>but</u> <u>it</u> can
                    A   B   C

    <u>to run</u> fast.
       D

    (A) (B) (C) (D)

6. <u>Do</u> students <u>has to</u> wear <u>uniforms</u> in high
     A   B   C

    schools <u>in Japan</u>?
             D

    (A) (B) (C) (D)

7. You <u>can</u> live for a few days without <u>food</u>,
         A   B

    but you <u>mustn't</u> live without <u>air</u> for more
             C   D

    than a few minutes.

    (A) (B) (C) (D)

8. Mozart <u>was able</u> to work very fast, and
            A

    <u>be able</u> to write <u>an opera</u> in just a few
       B   C

    <u>weeks</u>.
       D

    (A) (B) (C) (D)

9. <u>Penguins</u> <u>cannot</u> fly, but <u>they</u> <u>could</u> swim.
     A   B   C   D

    (A) (B) (C) (D)

10. "Walk in. No appointment necessary."

    <u>means</u> you <u>haven't</u> <u>to</u> make
     A   B   C

    <u>an appointment</u>.
       D

    (A) (B) (C) (D)

UNIT 12

SPECIAL EXPRESSIONS

12a *Let's*

Boy: Mom, I'm hungry.
Mother: Okay, **let's** go home.

Let's	*(Not)*	Base Verb
Let's	(not)	wait. sit down. go. eat.

Let's is a contraction of *let* + *us*. But we usually say and write *let's*.

Function

We use *let's* to make a suggestion for two or more people including the speaker.

It's cold. **Let's** close the window.
It's 12:30. **Let's** go to lunch.
Mother's birthday is next week. **Let's** not forget.

☐ Practice

Respond to the statements with *let's* or *let's not* and an expression from the list.

A.

buy some   eat now   go to a movie   hurry   take   walk

1. I love movies.

Okay. Let's go to a movie _____.

2. The movie theater isn't far away.

_____.

3. The movie starts in ten minutes.

_____.

4. My sister wants to go, too, but she's only five years old.

_____ her.

5. The popcorn smells good.

_____.

6. We are not hungry right now.

_____.

B.

clean up the apartment   make sandwiches   watch television
go to the beach   turn on the stereo

1. It's cold. We can't swim today.

_____.

2. There's a football game on TV in half an hour.

Great! _____.

3. I'm hungry. There's some bread and cheese.

_____.

4. I have a terrible headache!

_____.

5. Oh no! My parents are coming!

Quick! _____.

2 Practice

Work with a partner. Take turns and give responses with _let's_ or _let's not_.

Example:
You: Class starts in a few minutes.
Your partner: Let's not be late.

1. We have a test tomorrow.

2. It's a beautiful day.

3. We have ten minutes before class.

4. Next Monday is a holiday.

5. It's _____'s (name) birthday next week.

6. What do you want to do in class next lesson?

12b *Would Like*

Waiter: **Would you like** some cheese on your pasta?

Man:　　No, thank you.

STATEMENTS		
Subject	*Would Like*	Object
I You He She We They	**would like** **'d like**	a cup of tea.

YES/NO QUESTIONS				SHORT ANSWERS	
Would	Subject	*Like*	Object	**Yes,**	**No,**
Would	you he/she they	**like**	a cup of tea?	I/we **would.** he/she **would.** they **would.**	I/we **wouldn't.** he/she **wouldn't.** they **wouldn't.**

When a verb follows *would like*, we use the base form of the verb with *to*.

I'd like **to go** to Italy.
Would you like **to come**?

Note: We rarely use *Would I like...?* or *Would we like...?*

1. We use *would like* in place of want. *Would like* is more polite.

   I **want** a glass of water.   OR   I **would like** a glass of water. (polite)

2. *Would like* does not have the same meaning as *like*. Compare these sentences.

   I **would like** to go to the movies.   =   I want to go to the movies.
   I **like** to go to the movies.   =   I enjoy going to the movies.

---

3 Practice

Complete the dialogue with *would like*.

1. Waiter: _Would you like_____ a salad with your pasta?

   Mr. Lu: No, thanks.

2. Waiter: _____ a bottle of mineral water?

   Mr. Lu :   Just two glasses of regular water please.

3. Waiter: _____ some dessert?

   Mr. Lu: No, thank you.

4. Waiter: _____ some coffee?

   Mr. Lu: Yes, please.

5. Waiter: _____ espresso, cappuccino, or regular coffee?

   Mr. Lu: Two espressos please, and we _____ the check.

6. Waiter: _____ separate checks or one check?

   Mr. Lu: We _____ one check, please.

4 Practice

Read this list. Say if you'd like to or wouldn't like to do these things.

1. learn Chinese

   _I would like to learn Chinese_____.

2. become a teacher

   _____.

3. meet a movie star

   _____.

4. travel around the world

_____.

5. take a month off from school

_____.

6. become very rich

_____.

7. live in another country

_____.

8. have a motorcycle

_____.

9. have a short haircut

_____.

10. have an onion sandwich

_____.

11. have more homework

_____.

12. go to the Sahara desert

_____.

5 | Practice

Answer these questions with either _Yes/No, I would/wouldn't_ or _Yes/No, I do/don't._

1. Do you like to dance?

   Yes, I do _____.

2. Would you like to go dancing on Saturday?

   _____.

3. Do you like ice cream?

   _____.

4. Would you like to have ice cream after class?

   _____.

5. Do you like coffee?

   _____.

6. Would you like to have some coffee after class?

   _____.

7. Do you like pizza?

_____.

8. Would you like to have pizza tonight?

_____.

9. Do you like to read books?

_____.

10. Would you like more homework?

_____.

6 | Your Turn

A.
Work with a partner. Ask and answer these questions.

Example:
You: What do you like to watch on television?
Your partner: I like to watch mysteries and music videos.

1. What do you like to watch on television?

2. Where would you like to go on vacation?

3. What would you like to be?

4. What do you like to eat?

5. What don't you like to eat?

6. Where would you like to live?

7. Where wouldn't you like to live?

8. What kind of car would you like to have?

9. When do you like to go to bed?

10. What do you like to do in your free time?

11. What would you like to do after class?

12. Who would you like to meet one day?

B.
Tell the class about your partner.

Example:
My partner likes to go to the beach on her vacations.
She likes to eat fish, but she doesn't like beef.

12c *Could You* and *Would You*

Could you call me back in a few minutes? My hands are full right now.

	QUESTIONS		SHORT ANSWERS
Would you/ Could you	Base Form		
Would you **Could you**	**open**	the door?	Certainly.
	pass	me the salt?	Of course.
	stop	that noise?	Sure./OK. (informal)

Function

Manager: **Could you please** give this to Brad?

Assistant: Certainly.

Would you (please) and *Could you (please)* are two forms of requests. They are a polite way of asking someone to do something. They have the same meaning.

7 Practice

Tom is picking up Mrs. Hardy at the airport. Use the prompts to write her requests.

1. carry my suitcase

   Could you please carry my suitcase?

2. open the car door

   _____

3. turn off the car radio

   _____

4. drive slowly

   _____

5. turn on the heat

   _____

6. speak louder/I can't hear you.

   _____

7. repeat that/I didn't understand.

   _____

8 Practice

Work with a partner. Make polite requests and give short answers with these cues.

Example:
lend me $10
You: Could you lend me $10?
Your partner: Sorry. I don't have $10 to give you. OR Sure. Here you are.

1. take a photo of me

2. give me a ride tomorrow

3. come to the passport office with me

4. fill out this form for me

5. tell me where to buy this book

6. help me with my homework

7. show me how to work this computer

8. tell me the time

12d The Imperative

Put your hands together above your head.
Bend to the right.
Keep your body straight.
Don't bend your knees.

AFFIRMATIVE		NEGATIVE		
Base Verb		*Don't*	Base Verb	
Smile!		**Don't**	**smile!**	
Open	the door.	**Don't**	**open**	the door.
Answer	the questions.	**Don't**	**answer**	the questions.
Be	on time.	**Don't**	**be**	late.

Function

We use the imperative:

1. To give instructions.
    Turn right at the corner.
    Take one tablet every four hours.
2. To give advice.
    Don't go there! It's dangerous.
    Get some rest.
3. To give orders or tell people what to do.
    Sit down!   **Stop!**   **Don't talk!**
4. To make requests (with *please*).
    Come in, please.
    Please **close** the door.

9 Practice

Put these instructions in the correct order.

1. Dial the number. Lift the telephone receiver. Wait for the dial tone.

Lift the telephone receiver. Wait for the dial tone. Dial the number.

2. Write the letter. Mail it. Address the envelope. Put the letter in the envelope. Put a stamp on it. Sign your name.

_____

_____

_____

3. Cut the oranges in half. Buy some fresh oranges. Throw away the seeds and pulp. Add a little sugar, if you wish. Drink. Squeeze the halves until all the juice is out.

_____

_____

_____

_____

10 Practice

A.
Parents tell their children what to do. Complete the blanks with an affirmative or a negative imperative. Use the verbs in the list.

be	come	eat	talk	watch
brush	do	look	wash	

1. _Do_____ your homework.

2. _____ before you cross the street.

3. _____ your hands before you eat.

4. _____ home after school.

5. _____ too much television!

6. _____ your teeth.

7. _____ late!

8. _____ to strangers.

9. _____ too much candy!

B.
Add two more of your own.

1. _____

2. _____

Work with a partner. Use the imperative to tell your partner how to do the following things. Then write what you told him or her to do.

Example:
take care of a cold

Go home. Drink lots of warm liquids like tea and soup .
Take Vitamin C or eat oranges. Take aspirin. Keep warm .
Stay in bed if possible. Don't go to work .

1. get to your house from school

_____.
_____.
_____.

2. lose weight

_____.
_____.
_____.

3. cook rice or pasta

_____.
_____.
_____.

4. prepare for a test

_____.
_____.
_____.

5. prepare for a job interview

_____.
_____.
_____.

Write instructions.

Step 1. Put these sentences in the correct order.

HOW TO MAKE COFFEE

_____ Fill the coffee pot with boiling water.
_____ Pour the coffee into a cup.
__1__ Fill the kettle with water.
_____ Put some coffee in a coffee pot.
_____ Boil the water.
_____ Leave it for a few minutes.

Step 2. Write the sentences from Step 1 in the correct order.

1. _____
2. _____
3. _____
4. _____
5. _____
6. _____

Step 3. Write sentences to show how you make tea or another drink.

1. _____
2. _____
3. _____
4. _____
5. _____
6. _____

Step 4. Rewrite your sentences from Step 3 in paragraph form. Write a title in three or four words. For more writing guidelines, see pages 190-195.

Step 5. Evaluate your paragraph.

Checklist
_____ Did you use verb tenses correctly?
_____ Did you give all of the steps needed to make the drink?
_____ Did you check the order of the steps?

Step 6. Work with a partner to edit your sentences. Correct spelling, punctuation, vocabulary, and grammar.

Step 7. Write your final copy.

SELF-TEST

A Choose the best answer, A, B, C, or D, to complete the sentence. Mark your answer by darkening the oval with the same letter.

1. _____ go to a restaurant on your birthday.

   A. May   Ⓐ Ⓑ Ⓒ Ⓓ
   B. Could
   C. Let's to
   D. Let's

2. _____ a glass of water, please.

   A. I like   Ⓐ Ⓑ Ⓒ Ⓓ
   B. I would
   C. I'd like
   D. I would to like

3. A: Would you like a cup of coffee?
   B: Yes, I _____.

   A. do   Ⓐ Ⓑ Ⓒ Ⓓ
   B. would
   C. would like
   D. like

4. _____ late!

   A. You don't be   Ⓐ Ⓑ Ⓒ Ⓓ
   B. Don't be
   C. Not be
   D. Not to be

5. _____ please?

   A. Can you me help   Ⓐ Ⓑ Ⓒ Ⓓ
   B. Could you help me
   C. May you help me
   D. Could you me help

6. _____ your passport!

   A. Forget not   Ⓐ Ⓑ Ⓒ Ⓓ
   B. Don't forget
   C. Don't forgetting
   D. Not forget

7. A: Would you give this to Mr. Black?
   B: _____.

   A. Yes, I can   Ⓐ Ⓑ Ⓒ Ⓓ
   B. Yes, I would give
   C. Certainly
   D. I would

8. _____ speak English when you were ten?

   A. Could you   Ⓐ Ⓑ Ⓒ Ⓓ
   B. Would you
   C. Are you able to
   D. You could

9. _____ be quiet, please?

   A. Must you   Ⓐ Ⓑ Ⓒ Ⓓ
   B. Should you
   C. Could you
   D. Would

10. _____ the movie.

   A. I'd like to see   Ⓐ Ⓑ Ⓒ Ⓓ
   B. I would to see
   C. I'd like saw
   D. I'd like see

B Find the underlined word or phrase, A, B, C, or D, that is incorrect. Mark your answer by darkening the oval with the same letter.

1. <u>Don't</u> <u>to breathe</u>. <u>Hold</u> <u>your</u> breath.
   A   B   C   D

   Ⓐ Ⓑ Ⓒ Ⓓ

2. <u>Could</u> you <u>to speak</u> English when you <u>were</u>
   A   B   C

   <u>ten years old</u>?
   D

   Ⓐ Ⓑ Ⓒ Ⓓ

3. <u>Would</u> <u>I</u> borrow <u>your</u> pen for <u>a moment</u>,
   A   B   C   D

   please?

   Ⓐ Ⓑ Ⓒ Ⓓ

4. <u>Could</u> you <u>please</u> <u>to repeat</u> that because I
   A   B   C

   <u>didn't</u> hear you.
   D

   Ⓐ Ⓑ Ⓒ Ⓓ

5. <u>May</u> you <u>please</u> <u>close</u> the window? <u>It's</u>
   A   B   C   D

   cold here.

   Ⓐ Ⓑ Ⓒ Ⓓ

6. <u>Would</u> <u>you</u> <u>mailing</u> this letter <u>for me</u>?
   A   B   C   D

   Ⓐ Ⓑ Ⓒ Ⓓ

7. <u>You</u> <u>look at</u> <u>that</u> airplane. <u>It's</u> flying very
   A   B   C   D

   fast.

   Ⓐ Ⓑ Ⓒ Ⓓ

8. <u>I</u> <u>would</u> like <u>eat</u> <u>a sandwich</u> for lunch.
   A B   C   D

   Ⓐ Ⓑ Ⓒ Ⓓ

9. <u>Could</u> <u>I</u> tell <u>me</u> <u>the time</u>?
   A   B   C   D

   Ⓐ Ⓑ Ⓒ Ⓓ

10. She <u>would</u> not <u>likes</u> <u>to be</u> <u>a movie star</u>.
    A   B   C   D

    Ⓐ Ⓑ Ⓒ Ⓓ

UNIT 13

ADJECTIVES AND ADVERBS

13a Adjectives and Nouns Used as Adjectives

It is a **beautiful** day.
The sky is **blue**. The air is **clean**.
The **white** mountains are **beautiful.**

1. Adjectives come before nouns.

2. Adjectives can also come after the verb *to be* and some other verbs like *seem*.

3. Adjectives have the same form for singular and plural nouns.

1. Adjectives describe nouns.

   Lin has a **big** smile.

2. Nouns can also describe other nouns. The noun that describes another noun is always singular, just like an adjective.

   She is holding a **coffee** cup.
   She is in the **student** cafeteria.

1 Practice

What are the following underlined words? Put an X beside Noun or Adjective.

1. Lin is a <u>good</u> student.   Noun _____   Adjective _X_

2. She is going to a new <u>university</u>.   Noun _____   Adjective _____

3. The university is <u>modern</u>.   Noun _____   Adjective _____

4. Her <u>favorite</u> subject is biology.   Noun _____   Adjective _____

5. She wants to be a <u>doctor</u>.   Noun _____   Adjective _____

6. She is a <u>pretty</u> girl.   Noun _____   Adjective _____

7. She has black <u>hair</u>.   Noun _____   Adjective _____

8. She is also a <u>kind</u> person.   Noun _____   Adjective _____

9. She always helps her <u>friends</u>.   Noun _____   Adjective _____

10. She is a <u>wonderful</u> daughter too. Noun _____   Adjective _____

2 Your Turn

Describe each photo using adjectives from the list or your own.

Example:
She seems sad.

dark   long   short   young
happy   sad   thick

3 Practice

Underline the nouns used as adjectives. There are thirteen nouns used as adjectives.

I went for a walk in the <u>city</u> center yesterday. There is a town hall in the center. On one side, there are office buildings and government offices. On the other side, there is a police station, a bus station, and a coffee shop. There is also a movie theater and an art gallery. In the center, there is a small park with big flower pots and park benches. Yesterday I saw a man near a telephone booth by one of the benches. He was waiting by the telephone. There was a cardboard box on the bench near him. I remember him because he looked very worried.

4 What Do You Think?

Why was the man waiting?
Did the box belong to him?

5 Practice

What are the following items? Complete the names of the objects with the words from the list.

coffee	key	paper	sun	tooth
light	note	perfume	tea	

1. _note_ pad.

2. _____ bulb.

3. _____ ring.

4. _____ pot.

5. _____ cup.

6. _____ bottle.

7. _____ glasses.

8. _____ clips.

9. _____ brush.

6 Practice

Work with a partner. Combine the word in capital letters with the words under it. You can put the word in front of or after the word in capital letters. Write the definition. Some combinations are two words; some are one. Check with your teacher or a dictionary.

1. SCHOOL

teacher _schoolteacher = a teacher at a school_

entrance _school entrance = an entrance of a school_

adult _adult school = a school for adults_

2. MONEY

paper _____

order _____

box _____

3. MUSIC

piano _____

concert _____

hall _____

4. HOUSE

keeper _____

work _____

country _____

5. BANK

account _____

statement _____

teller _____

6. WATER

sea _____

glass _____

mountain _____

7. PAINT

brush _____

store _____

oil _____

8. TABLE

kitchen _____

manners _____

tennis _____

9. CLASS

computer _____

history _____

schedule _____

10. DAY

time _____

break _____

birth _____

13b Word Order of Adjectives

She has **beautiful brown** eyes.
She has **long brown curly** hair.

When we use two or more adjectives, we use this general order.

	1. Opinion	2. Size	3. Age	5. Color	6. Material	7. Nationality	
	beautiful						
	beautiful	large					
It's a	beautiful	large	old				box.
	beautiful	large	old	red			
	beautiful	large	old	red	wooden		
	beautiful	large	old	red	wooden	Chinese	

Note: We do not usually use more than two or three adjectives with one noun.

7 Practice

Tina's apartment was robbed. Tina gave this list to the police. Circle *a* or *an* and put the adjectives in the correct order.

1. gold/new   (a)/an _____ *new gold* _____ credit card

2. diamond/interesting   a/an _____ bracelet

3. beautiful/Chinese/old   a/an _____ plate

4. Japanese/new/small   a/an _____ computer

5. leather/black/beautiful   a/an _____ purse

6. gold/old/Swiss   a/an _____ watch

7. expensive/big/blue   a/an _____ ring

8. Persian/silk/old   a/an _____ carpet

9. white/Japanese/pearl   a/an _____ necklace

10. silver/antique/English   a/an _____ jewelry box

8 Practice

Complete the sentences with words from the list.

| American | cotton | leather | note | red |
| apple | interesting | modern | quiet | rose |

Ted is a _____ *quiet* _____ young man. He lives alone in a _____
        1   **2**

brick house. The house has one bedroom with a single bed with clean white

_____ sheets. It has a bright _____ kitchen. From the
    3   **4**

kitchen window you can see a beautiful _____ garden and an old
                                          5

_____ tree. In the office, there is a black _____ sofa and
    6   **7**

an _____ old desk. On the desk, there is a telephone, a small computer
   8

and a _____ pad. There are books everywhere. There are also old
      9

_____ newspapers, mostly the *New York Times*.
    10

9 What Do You Think?

What can you say about Ted?

10 Your Turn

A.

Use two adjectives or nouns used as adjectives to describe the following items.

Example:
your shoes
You: I'm wearing comfortable brown shoes.

1. your shoes

2. your house or apartment

3. your camera

4. your watch

5. your eyes

6. your partner in class

B.

Write a paragraph describing a person in your class. Use adjectives.

_____

_____

_____

_____

_____

_____

_____

_____

13c *The Same (As), Similar (To),* and *Different (From)*

Photo A   Photo B

Photos A and B are **the same.**
A is **the same as** B.

Photo L   Photo M

Photos L and M **are similar.**
L is **similar to** M.

Photo X   Photo Y

Photos X and Y are **different.**
X is **different from** Y.

11 Practice

Which photos are the same, similar, or different?

Photo A   Photo B   Photo C   Photo D

1. Photo C and Photo D are _____*the same*_____.

2. Photo B and Photo C are _____.

3. Photo D is _____ Photo C.

4. Photo B is _____ Photo C.

5. Photo A is _____ Photo C.

6. Photo B and Photo D are _____.

12 Practice

Look at the printing. Which is the same, similar, or different?

Line 1: **To be or not to be**   Line 4: TO BE OR NOT TO BE

Line 2: **To be or not to be**   Line 5: TO BE OR NOT TO BE

Line 3: *To be or not to be*   Line 6: **TO BE OR NOT TO BE**

1. Line 1 is ____*the same as*____ Line 2.

2. Line 2 and Line 1 are _____.

3. Line 3 is _____ Line 2.

4. Line 3 is _____ Line 4.

5. Line 3 and Line 4 are _____.

6. Line 4 and Line 5 are _____.

7. Line 5 is _____ Line 4.

8. Line 5 is _____ Line 6.

9. Lines 5 and 6 are _____.

Name three people and three things in your classroom that are the same, similar, or different. Use complete sentences.

Example:
X and I have the same book.
X and I have similar hair.
X and I have different eyes.   OR   My eyes are different from X's.

13d *Like* and *Alike*

The daughter's mouth **is like** her mother's mouth.
The daughter's and mother's mouths **are alike**.

1. *Like* and *alike* have the same meaning.

2. *Like* is a preposition. It means "similar to."

Subject	*Be*	*Like*	Object
The daughter	**is**	**like**	the mother.

3. *Alike* is an adjective. It means "similar."

Subject	*Be*	*Alike*
The mother and daughter	**are**	**alike.**

14 Practice

Complete the sentences with *like* and *alike*.

Terry   Jerry

1. Terry and Jerry have similar faces. Their faces are ____*alike*____.

2. Terry and Jerry have similar names. Terry's name is _____ Jerry's name.

3. Terry and Jerry wear a similar style of clothes. Terry's clothes are _____ Jerry's clothes.

4. Terry and Jerry have similar cars. Their cars are _____.

5. Terry and Jerry have similar jobs. Terry's job is _____ Jerry's job.

6. Terry and Jerry live in similar apartments. Jerry's apartment is _____ Terry's apartment.

7. Terry and Jerry have similar friends. Their friends are _____.

8. Terry and Jerry have similar lives. Terry's life is _____ Jerry's life.

15 What Do You Think?

Which of these things are similar? Why? Use *like* in your answers.

Example:
A chicken is similar to a turkey. They are both birds.

blouse	guitar	shirt	turkey
chicken	New York	Tokyo	violin

13e Comparative Form of Adjectives: *-er* and *More*

Monica's house   Olivia's house

Monica's house is **bigger than** Olivia's house.
Olivia's house is **older than** Monica's house.
Monica's house is **more expensive than** Olivia's house.

When we compare things, we use a comparative adjective + *than*.

1. Short adjectives (one syllable): Add *-er*.

Adjective	Comparative Adjective
long	long**er than**
old	old**er than**
hot	hot**ter* than**

* If an adjective ends in one vowel and one consonant, double the consonant.

2. One and two syllable adjectives ending in *y*: Change *y* to *i* and add *-er*.

Adjective	Comparative Adjective
happy	happ**ier than**
hungry	hungr**ier than**
friendly	friendl**ier than**

3. Long adjectives (two syllables or more): Use *more* in front of the adjective.

Adjective	Comparative Adjective
difficult	**more** difficult **than**
expensive	**more** expensive **than**
beautiful	**more** beautiful **than**

4. Irregular adjectives:

Adjective	Comparative Adjective
good	**better than**
bad	**worse than**
far	**farther/further than**

16 Practice

Write the comparative form of the adjective.

1. small   _smaller than_

2. big

3. hot

4. cold

5. good

6. bad

7. strong

8. interesting

9. funny

10. young

11. weak

12. pretty

13. thin

14. famous

15. far

16. sad

17 **Practice**

Complete the sentences about Karen and Connie. Use the comparative form of the words in parentheses.

Karen
140 pounds (63.5 kilograms)
5 feet 5 inches (165 centimeters)
friendly
34 years old

Connie
110 pounds (50 kilograms)
5 feet 2 inches (157 centimeters)
quiet
28 years old

1. Karen is (old) _*older than*_ Connie.

2. Connie is (young) _____ Karen.

3. Karen is (tall) _____ Connie.

4. Connie is (small) _____ Karen.

5. Connie is (thin) _____ Karen.

6. Karen is (heavy) _____ Connie.

7. Connie's hair is (dark) _____ Karen.

8. Connie is (quiet) _____ Karen.

9. Karen is (friendly) _____ Connie.

18 **Practice**

Complete the sentences about London and New York. Use the comparative form of the words in parentheses.

London
Population: 6.7 million
Temperatures: 39–64°F / 4–18°C
Rain: 610 mm. / 24 inches

New York
Population: 8.0 million
Temperatures: 30–73°F / -1–23°C
Rain: 1,123 mm. / 44 inches

1. London is (old) _____older than_____ New York.

2. New York is (crowded) _____ London.

3. London is (small) _____ New York in population.

4. The buildings in New York are (tall) _____ the buildings in London.

5. New York is (exciting) _____ London.

6. The buildings in New York are (modern) _____ the buildings in London.

7. Life in New York is (fast) _____ life in London.

8. The summer in New York is (hot) _____ the summer in London.

9. London is (rainy) _____ New York.

10. The museums in London are (interesting) _____ the museums in New York.

11. London is (expensive) _____ New York.

12. People in London drive (slow) _____ people in New York.

19 What Do You Think?

Do you prefer London or New York? Why?

20 Practice

Look again at Monica's house and Olivia's house on page 136. Compare the houses using the adjectives below.

1. small   _Olivia's house is smaller than Monica's house_____.

2. old   _____.

3. big   _____.

4. modern   _____.

5. expensive _____.

6. luxurious _____.

7. new   _____.

8. spacious   _____.

21 Your Turn

With a partner, discuss which house you prefer and why.

Example:
I prefer Olivia's house because it is older.

13f *As...As, Not As...As, and Less...Than*

Mark　　　　　　**Joe**

Mark is **as tall as** Joe. = Mark and Joe are the same height.

Mark is **as old as** Joe. = Mark and Joe are the same age.

Mark isn**'t as trendy as** Joe. = Joe is more trendy. Mark is less trendy.

	As	Adjective	*As*	
Mark is	**as**	**tall** **old**	**as**	Joe.
	Not As	Adjective	*As*	
Mark is	**not as**	**trendy** **casual**	**as**	Joe.
	Less	Adjective	*Than*	
Mark is	**less**	**trendy** **casual**	**than**	Joe.

Function

1. We use *as...as* to show that two things or people are the same in some way.

2. We use *not as...as* to show that two things are different in some way.

3. We use *less...than* with a long adjective (two syllables or more), except for two-syllable adjectives ending in *y*.

   Joe **isn't as conservative as** Mark. = Joe is **less conservative than** Mark.

4. We do not use *less...than* with one-syllable adjectives.

   CORRECT:　　Mark isn't as tall as Joe.
   INCORRECT:　Mark ~~is less tall than~~ Joe.

22 Practice

Complete the sentences with _as...as_ and the adjectives in parentheses.

Mark's car   **Joe's car**

1. Mark's car is (old) _____ _as old as_ _____ Joe's car.

2. Joe's car isn't (clean) _____ Mark's car.

3. Joe's car isn't (large) _____ Mark's car.

4. Joe's car isn't (luxurious) _____ Mark's car.

5. Joe's car isn't (quiet) _____ Mark's car.

6. Mark's car isn't (trendy) _____ Joe's car.

7. Mark's car isn't (sporty) _____ Joe's car.

8. Mark's car isn't (strong) _____ Joe's car.

23 Practice

A.
Rewrite the sentences to have the same meaning, using *less* where possible. Write "No change" if it isn't possible to use *less*.

1. Mark's life isn't as fun as Joe's life.

   no change .

2. Joe's office isn't as luxurious as Mark's office.

   Joe's office is less luxurious than Mark's office .

3. Joe's life isn't as complicated as Mark's life.

   _____ .

4. Mark's life isn't as exciting as Joe's life.

   _____ .

5. Joe's clothes aren't as expensive as Mark's clothes.

   _____ .

6. Mark's clothes aren't as fashionable as Joe's clothes.

   _____ .

7. Joe's house isn't as sophisticated as Mark's house.

   _____ .

8. Mark's house isn't as trendy as Joe's house.

   _____ .

B.
Joe is a musician. Mark is a banker. Make a sentence about Joe's life or Mark's life with *as...as* or *not as...as*.

_____

Many expressions in English use *as...as*. Look at the pictures and complete the expressions.

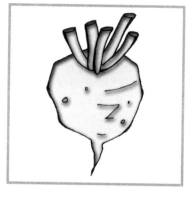

a beet

a picture

ice

a bee

a bear

an ox

1. Jamie is always working. She never stops. She is as busy as _____*a bee*_____.

2. Tony can carry the suitcases for you. He is as strong as _____.

3. Bill didn't eat all day. He was very hungry. He was as hungry as _____.

4. Melanie looked pretty in her new dress. She was as pretty as _____.

5. Helen didn't look well. Her face was white, and her hands were as cold

    as _____.

6. Tina is very shy. She is in front of the class. Everyone is looking at her. Her face is as

    red as _____.

25 Your Turn

Tell a classmate about the expressions in your language to make comparisons.
Are they similar to the ones in this chapter?

Example:

In my language, we make the comparative with...

26 Practice

Write sentences with the same meaning using *as...as.*

The Victoria Motel

The Palace Hotel

1. The room at the Victoria is smaller than the room at the Palace.

   The room isn't as big as the room at the Palace .

2. The Victoria is less expensive than the Palace.

   _____ .

3. The bed in the Victoria is less comfortable than the bed in the Palace.

   _____ .

4. The Palace is farther away from the city center.

   _____ .

5. The hotel service at the Victoria is worse than at the Palace.

   _____ .

6. The Victoria is more crowded than the Palace.

_____.

7. The coffee at the Victoria is weaker than the coffee at the Palace.

_____.

8. The Victoria is less modern than the Palace.

_____.

9. The furniture at the Victoria is older than the furniture at the Palace.

_____.

10. The restaurant at the Palace is better than the restaurant at the Victoria.

_____.

27 Practice

What can you say about the Palace Hotel? Use one of the comparative forms of the adjectives from the list or use your own.

comfortable   expensive   good   nice   quiet

Example:
The Palace Hotel is better than the Victoria Hotel.

1. _____

_____.

2. _____

_____.

3. _____

_____.

4. _____

_____.

5. _____

_____.

13g Superlative Form of Adjectives: -est and Most

Vatican City is **the smallest** country in the world.
It has **the oldest** army.
It has **the most famous** church in the world.
St. Peter's is **the largest** and **most beautiful** church in the world.

We form superlative adjectives with *-est* or *most*.

	Adjective	Comparative	Superlative
Short adjectives	long	long**er** (than)	**the** long**est**
	cheap	cheap**er** (than)	**the** cheap**est**
Two syllable adjectives ending in *y*	happy	happ**ier** (than)	**the** happ**iest**
	heavy	heav**ier** (than)	**the** heav**iest**
Two or more syllable adjectives	famous	**more** famous (than)	**the most** famous
	difficult	**more** difficult (than)	**the most** difficult
Irregular adjectives	good	**better** (than)	**the best**
	bad	**worse** (than)	**the worst**
	far	**farther/further** (than)	**the farthest/furthest**

We use *the* + the superlative form of an adjective (+ *of* or *in*) to compare three or more people or things.

Sue is **the most talented of** the three sisters.
Vatican City is **the smallest** country **in** the world.

28 Practice

Write the superlative form of the following adjectives.

1. cold   _the coldest_
2. sad   _____
3. hungry   _____
4. wet   _____
5. useful   _____
6. intelligent   _____
7. near   _____
8. easy   _____

9. good   _____
10. bad   _____
11. far   _____
12. boring   _____
13. popular   _____
14. nice   _____
15. high   _____
16. friendly   _____

29 Practice

Complete the geography facts with the correct form of the adjective in parentheses.

1. Vatican City is (small) _the smallest_ country in the world.
2. The Nile is (long) _____ river in the world.
3. Mount Everest is (high) _____ mountain in the world.
4. Antarctica is (cold) _____ continent in the world.
5. Asia is (big) _____ continent in the world.
6. The Dead Sea is (salty) _____ sea in the world.
7. The Pacific Ocean is (large) _____ ocean in the world.
8. The Pacific Ocean is (deep) _____ ocean in the world.
9. The Sahara Desert is (hot) _____ desert in the world.
10. Hawaii is the (wet) _____ place in the world.

Practice

Complete the sentences about places with the correct form of the adjective in parentheses.

1. The CN Tower in Canada was (tall) _____*the tallest*_____ building in the world in 2004.

2. The Taj Mahal is (beautiful) _____ building in the world.

3. The Nova Hotel in Paris, France, is (expensive) _____ hotel in the world.

4. The Eiffel Tower in Paris is (famous) _____ building in France.

5. Mexico City is (crowded) _____ city in the world.

6. Urungu, a city in China, is (far) _____ city from the sea.

7. Jericho in Jordan is (old) _____ city in the world.

8. Heathrow Airport in London is (busy) _____ airport in the world.

9. The White House in Washington, D.C., is (important) _____ house in the United States.

10. Los Angeles, California, has (good) _____ freeway system in the world.

31 Practice

Make true sentences using the comparative and superlative form of adjectives from the list. Use each word two times.

heavy   old   short   tall   thin   young

Ken   Paul   Brad

1. Ken is _____*younger than*_____ Paul.

2. Ken is _____ of all.

3. Paul is _____ Brad.

4. Paul is _____ of all.

5. Ken is _____ Paul.

6. Ken is _____ of all.

7. Paul is _____ Ken.

8. Paul is _____ of all.

9. Brad is _____ Paul.

10. Brad is _____ of all.

11. Brad is _____ Ken.

12. Brad is _____ of all.

32 Your Turn

With a partner, ask and answer questions about your country. Give complete answers.

Example:
You: Which is the biggest city in Japan?
Your partner: Tokyo is the biggest city in Japan.

Which is...

1. the biggest city

2. the largest airport

3. the busiest street

4. the oldest building

5. the coldest month

6. the hottest month

7. the wettest month

8. the most beautiful building

13h *One Of The* + Superlative + Plural Noun

Form

The Mona Lisa is **one of the most famous** paintings in the world.

It is in **one of the biggest** museums in the world, the Louvre, in Paris, France.

	One Of	Superlative	Plural Noun	
It is		**the biggest**	stores	in the city.
He is	**one of**	**the richest**	men	in the world.
They are		**the most powerful**	families	in the town.

33 Practice

Write sentences using the prompts and *one of the* + superlative + plural noun.

1. the Taj Mahal/beautiful building/in the world *The Taj Mahal is one of the most beautiful buildings in the world* .

2. the Beatles/successful rock band/in the world _____
   _____ .

3. Siberia/cold place/in the world _____
   _____ .

4. California/large state/in the United States _____
   _____ .

5. Egypt/interesting country/to visit _____
   _____ .

6. the computer/great invention/of our time _____

_____ .

7. New York/important city/in the United States _____

_____ .

8. Mont Blanc/high mountain/in the world _____

_____ .

9. the Sears Tower in Chicago/tall building/in the world _____

_____ .

10. Tokyo/crowded city/in the world _____

_____ .

11. a racehorse/fast animal/in the world _____

_____ .

12. boxing/dangerous sport/in the world _____

_____ .

34 Practice

Work with a partner. Make questions for these answers. Use words from the list or add your own.

| beautiful | cold | long | strong |
| big | important | popular | sweet |

1. _What is one of the most popular hot drinks in Asia_____ ?

Tea.

2. _____ ?

Tokyo.

3. _____ ?

The Amazon River.

4. _____ ?

The lion.

5. _____ ?

Oxford University.

6. _____ ?

Soccer.

7. _____?

Pizza.

8. _____?

Honey.

9. _____?

Paris.

10. _____?

The North Pole.

13i Adjectives and Adverbs

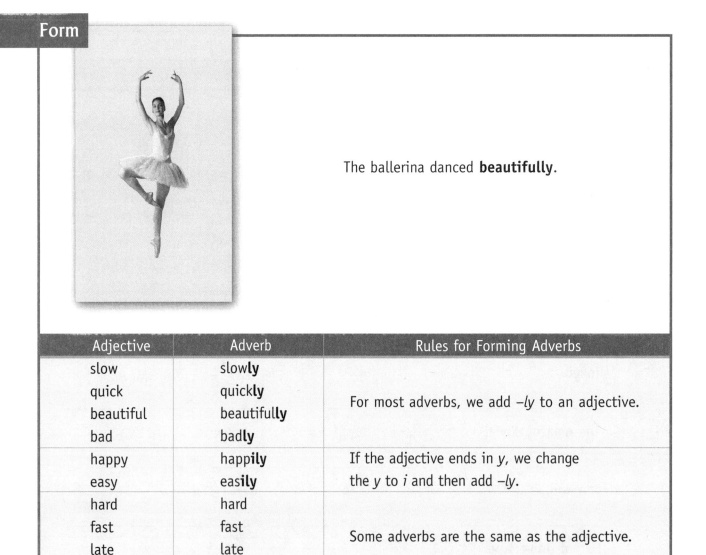

Form

The ballerina danced **beautifully**.

Adjective	Adverb	Rules for Forming Adverbs
slow	slow**ly**	For most adverbs, we add –_ly_ to an adjective.
quick	quick**ly**	
beautiful	beautiful**ly**	
bad	bad**ly**	
happy	happ**ily**	If the adjective ends in _y_, we change the _y_ to _i_ and then add –_ly_.
easy	eas**ily**	
hard	hard	Some adverbs are the same as the adjective.
fast	fast	
late	late	
early	early	
good	well	The adverb form of _good_ is _well_.

Adjectives and adverbs look similar, but they do different things.

1. An adjective describes a noun and usually answers the question *what*.

   What color is the car? The car is **red**.

2. An adverb often answers the question *how*. Adverbs describe verbs, adjectives, and other adverbs.

   How does she dance? She dances **beautifully**. She dances **very beautifully.**

35 Practice

Put the following words into the correct column.

carefully	easily	good	noisy
dangerous	fast	hard	quietly
early	funny	late	slowly

Adjective	Adverb	Adjective or Adverb
noisy		

36 Read

Read about Janet. Underline the adverbs. Then answer the questions.

> Janet is a <u>very</u> careful person. She gets to work on time and does everything perfectly. She works hard at home and at work. She drives her car to work. She drives carefully. She doesn't drive fast, and she stops at all the red lights. But, on her way home yesterday evening, she drove badly and almost had an accident.

1. What kind of person is Janet? _She is a careful person_ .

2. Does she work hard? _____ .

3. How does she usually drive? _____ .

4. How did she drive yesterday evening? _____ .

5. Did she have an accident? _____ .

37   What Do You Think ?

Why do you think Janet drove badly yesterday?

38   Practice

Susan is the best person for this job. Here's why. Underline the correct form of the adjective or adverb.

1. She speaks English very (good/<u>well</u>).
2. She is very (polite/politely) to people.
3. She gets along with people (easy/easily).
4. She is a (hard/hardly) worker.
5. She is a (good/well) writer.
6. She types (fast/fastly) on the computer.
7. She is very (careful/carefully) with her work.
8. She keeps the office (clean/cleanly).
9. She dresses (nice/nicely).
10. She is never (late/lately).
11. She is always (happy/happily).
12. But you must pay her (generous/generously)!

39   Practice

English is very important for me. Underline the correct form of the adjective or adverb.

1. I want to have a (<u>good</u>/well) English accent.
2. I want to speak English (fluent/fluently).
3. I want to read an English newspaper (quick/quickly).
4. I want to understand people (good/well).
5. I want to be an (excellent/excellently) student in my English class.
6. I want to know my past participles (perfect/perfectly).
7. I want to spell words (correct/correctly).
8. I want to write in English (easy/easily).
9. I want to understand English grammar (complete/completely).
10. I want to learn English (fast/fastly)!

From the sentences in Practice 39, which three things do you want most of all?

Example:
I want to speak English well.

13j Comparative and Superlative Forms of Adverbs

Form

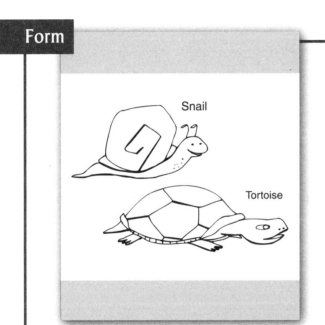

Snail

Tortoise

A snail moves **more slowly** than a tortoise.
A snail moves **more silently** than a tortoise.
In fact, the snail moves **the most slowly** of
all animals.

Adverb	Comparative	Superlative	
easily	**more** easily	**the most** easily	We compare adverbs ending in *ly* with *more* and *the most*.
slowly	**more** slowly	**the most** slowly	
carefully	**more** carefully	**the most** carefully	
fast	fast**er**	the fast**est**	For adverbs which have the same form as adjectives, we add *–er* and *-est*.
hard	hard**er**	the hard**est**	
early	earl**ier**	the earl**iest**	
well	better	the best	*Well* is an irregular adverb.

41 Practice

Complete the sentences using the comparative form of the adverbs in italics. Veronica thinks she is better at doing certain things than Karen. This is what Veronica thinks.

1. Karen learns English *easily*, but I learn it _____ *more easily* _____.

2. Karen dresses *fashionably*, but I dress _____.

3. Karen runs *fast*, but I run _____.

4. Karen works *hard*, but I work _____.

5. Karen learns *quickly*, but I learn _____.

6. Karen speaks French *fluently*, but I speak French _____.

7. Karen cooks *well*, but I cook _____.

8. Karen gets up *early*, but I get up _____.

9. Karen speaks *carefully*, but I speak _____.

42 What Do You Think?

Look at the three women. Who is going to be the new manager? Why?
Use the adjectives or adverbs in the list to write comparative and superlative sentences.

careful/carefully	fast/faster	hard/harder	old/young
early/late	friendly*	longer	slower/slowly

* *Friendly* looks like an adverb, but it is really an adjective that ends in *ly*.

Lydia
Age: 49
Experience: 20 years
• gets to work early
• works carefully
• writes reports a little late
• works fast
• works 9 hours a day
• friendly at times

Sue
Age: 34
Experience: 2 years
• gets to work on time
• works very carefully
• writes reports on time
• works very fast
• works 8 hours a day
• friendly all the time

Gina
Age: 29
Experience: 5 years
• gets to work late
• not careful
• writes reports late
• works slowly
• works 6 hours a day
• very friendly and happy person

1. *Sue is the most careful* _____ .

2. _____ .

3. _____ .

4. _____ .

5. _____ .

6. _____ .

7. _____ .

8. _____ .

43 Your Turn

A.

Think about three bosses or teachers from your past. Tell your partner about them. Use superlative adverbs.

Example:
Ms. Taheri was my best teacher. She taught us the most successfully of all the teachers.

B.

Write three things that your partner said about his or her bosses or teachers.

_____

_____

_____

_____

_____

_____

_____

_____

_____

13k *As...As* with Adverbs

Alex

Mike

Alex doesn't dress **as neatly as** Mike.

	As	Adverb	*As*	
Tony speaks English		**fluently**		John (does).
Karen runs	**as**	**fast**	**as**	Jan (does).
Mary and Jane work		**hard**		John and Pete (do).

1. When things are the same, we put *as...as* around the adverb.

   She worked **as fast as** a machine.

2. We can also follow *as* + adverb + *as* with a subject and a form of the verb *do* or modals like *can* or *could*.

   He worked **as fast as I did.**
   He worked **as fast as he could.**

3. We use the negative form *not as...as* to show things are not the same.

   Alex does**n't** study **as hard as** Mike.

44 Practice

Alex and Mike are friends, but they are different in many ways. Complete the sentences.

1. Alex doesn't work as hard _____*as*_____ Mike _____*does*_____ .

2. He doesn't get up as early _____ Mike _____ .

3. Mike doesn't go to bed as late _____ Alex _____ .

4. Alex doesn't work as quickly _____ Mike _____ .

5. Mike doesn't play sports as well _____ Alex and his friends _____ .

6. Alex doesn't talk as politely _____ Mike and his friends _____ .

7. Mike doesn't dress as casually _____ Alex and his friends _____ .

8. Alex doesn't drive as carefully _____ Mike _____ .

45 Practice

The students have a big test tomorrow. The teacher is giving advice to the students. Change the sentences to *as...as + can*.

1. get up/early   *Get up as early as you can* _____ .

2. study/hard   _____ .

3. come to school/early _____ .

4. read the instructions/carefully _____ .

5. answer the questions/well _____ .

6. write/fast   _____ .

7. write/neatly   _____ .

8. finish/soon   _____ .

WRITING: Write a Paragraph of Comparison

Write a paragraph of comparison.

Step 1. A friend is coming to your city to study English. He/She wants you to find out
about English schools. Your friend would like to be in the city center. Cost is no problem.
Read the information about the three language schools. With a partner, compare the
three schools.

Name	Age	Price	Location	Test Pass Rate	Students in Class
Achieve Language Center	25 years	$1,200	Suburbs	75%	15
City School of English	2 years	$1,500	Downtown	40%	25
English Language Institute	15 years	$1,700	Downtown	60%	20

Step 2. Write sentences that compare the schools.

Step 3. Rewrite your sentences as a paragraph in the letter below. For more writing
guidelines, see pages 190-195.

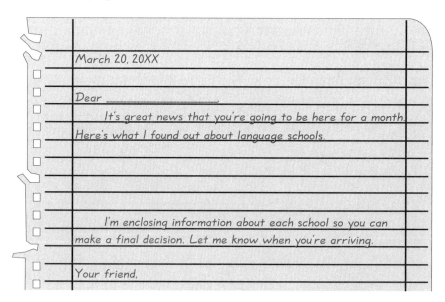

March 20, 20XX

Dear _____,

   It's great news that you're going to be here for a month.
Here's what I found out about language schools.

   I'm enclosing information about each school so you can
make a final decision. Let me know when you're arriving.

Your friend,

Step 4. Edit your paragraph. Correct spelling, punctuation, vocabulary, and grammar.

Step 5. Write your final copy.

SELF-TEST

A **Choose the best answer, A, B, C, or D, to complete the sentence. Mark your answer by darkening the oval with the same letter.**

1. Tony's English _____.

   A. like mine   Ⓐ Ⓑ Ⓒ Ⓓ
   B. like me
   C. is like mine
   D. alike mine

2. The new television show is _____ than the old show.

   A. more funny   Ⓐ Ⓑ Ⓒ Ⓓ
   B. funnier
   C. funniest
   D. the funnier

3. New York is _____ Tokyo.

   A. less crowded as   Ⓐ Ⓑ Ⓒ Ⓓ
   B. least crowded
   C. less crowded than
   D. less crowdeder than

4. It's _____ store in town.

   A. most expensive   Ⓐ Ⓑ Ⓒ Ⓓ
   B. the expensivest
   C. the most expensive
   D. the more expensive

5. He ran _____ he could.

   A. as quicker as   Ⓐ Ⓑ Ⓒ Ⓓ
   B. as quickly as
   C. quickly as
   D. as quickest as

6. Your English is _____ mine.

   A. fluenter than   Ⓐ Ⓑ Ⓒ Ⓓ
   B. fluent than
   C. more fluenter than
   D. more fluent than

7. His car _____ my car.

   A. is the same as   Ⓐ Ⓑ Ⓒ Ⓓ
   B. is the same
   C. same
   D. is as same as

8. Ted's job is _____ my father's job.

   A. similar as   Ⓐ Ⓑ Ⓒ Ⓓ
   B. similar from
   C. the similar as
   D. similar to

9. He is a _____ man.

   A. Chinese, tall, young   Ⓐ Ⓑ Ⓒ Ⓓ
   B. young, tall, Chinese
   C. tall, young, Chinese
   D. Chinese, young, tall

10. I bought a pair of _____ shoes.

    Ⓐ Ⓑ Ⓒ Ⓓ

    A. black, leather, comfortable
    B. leather, comfortable, black
    C. comfortable, black, leather
    D. comfortable, leather, black

B Find the underlined word or phrase, A, B, C, or D, that is incorrect. Mark your answer by darkening the oval with the same letter.

1. <u>Electricity</u> is <u>one of the</u> <u>importantest</u>
   A   B   C

   <u>inventions</u> in the world.
   D

2. <u>The elephant</u> <u>is</u> the <u>bigger</u> land <u>animal</u> in
   A   B   C   D

   the world.

3. The Forbidden City in China <u>is</u> <u>the most</u>
                                A   B

   <u>largest</u> palace <u>in the world</u>.
   C   D

4. The CN Tower <u>in</u> Toronto, Canada, <u>is</u>
                 A   B

   <u>more taller</u> <u>than</u> the Sears Tower in
   C   D

   Chicago.

5. The Louvre Museum in Paris is <u>one of the</u>
                                  A   B

   <u>famousest</u> <u>museums</u> in the world.
   C   D

6. A cup of Italian espresso coffee <u>is</u> <u>more</u>
                                     A   B

   <u>stronger</u> <u>than</u> a cup of American coffee.
   C   D

7. The world's <u>tallest</u> and <u>most</u> <u>shortest</u> <u>people</u>
               A   B   C   D

   live in Africa.

8. The blue whale is <u>the</u> <u>largest</u> animal in
                      A   B

   the world and it is <u>as</u> heavy <u>than</u> about
                       C   D

   1,800 people.

9. A newborn African elephant <u>is</u> two times
                               A

   <u>as</u> heavy <u>than</u> <u>an</u> adult human.
   B   C   D

10. The <u>most</u> <u>fastest</u> <u>animals</u> in the world <u>are</u>
        A   B   C   D

   birds.

162

Unit 13

UNIT 14

THE PRESENT PERFECT TENSE

14a The Present Perfect Tense of *Be*: *For* and *Since*

Carlos **has been** a waiter for six months.

We form the present perfect tense of *be* with *have* or *has* and the past participle of the verb *be*.

AFFIRMATIVE STATEMENT			
Subject	*Have/Has*	Past Participle of *Be*	
I You	**have**		
He She It	**has**	**been**	here **for** two hours. **since** 10 o'clock.
We You They	**have**		

YES/NO QUESTIONS			SHORT ANSWERS	
Have/Has	Subject	Past Participle of *Be*	Affirmative	Negative
			Yes,	**No,**
	I		you **have.**	you **haven't.**
Have	you		I/we **have.**	I/we **haven't.**
	we		you **have.**	you **haven't.**
	they	**been** here?	they **have.**	they **haven't.**
	he		he **has.**	he **hasn't.**
Has	she		she **has.**	she **hasn't.**
	it		it **has.**	it **hasn't.**

CONTRACTIONS			
Subject Pronoun + *Have/Has*		*Have/Has* + Not	
I have	**I've**	I have**n't**	
you have	**you've**	you have**n't**	
he has	**he's**	he has**n't**	
she has	**she's**	she has**n't**	
it has	**it's**	it has**n't**	
we have	**we've**	we have**n't**	
they have	**they've**	they have**n't**	

Note: In the contractions *he's, she's,* and *it's,* the *'s* can stand for either *has* or *is*. The sentence structure tells which one it is.

Lin and Sue have been friends for four years.

1. We can use the present perfect tense to talk about an action or situation that started in the past and continues up to the present.

2. We often use the present perfect with *for* and *since*.

165

3. We use *for* and *since* with the present perfect to talk about how long the action or situation existed from the past to the present. We use *for* to talk about a length of time; we use *since* to talk about when a period of time began.

	For		Since
for	four years	**since**	1990
	six months		last year
	five weeks		(last) June
	four days		(last) Friday
	three hours		yesterday
	twenty minutes		this morning
	a minute		nine o'clock this morning
	a long time		I moved to Tokyo

1 Practice

Complete the sentences with the present perfect of the verb *be*.

1. Sue and Lin met at the university four years ago. They ___*have been*___ friends for four years.

2. Lin married Steve last April. She _____ married since April.

3. Lin and Steve bought a new home last June. They _____ in the new house since June.

4. They _____ very happy in their new home since they moved in.

5. Life _____ very good for them since they got married.

6. Sue works part time in a lab. She _____ a chemist for ten months now.

7. Sue has a new boss. She _____ very happy since he became her boss.

8. Sue also moved to a new apartment with her sister this month. They _____ _____ in the apartment for only three weeks.

9. Sue _____ busy since the beginning of the month.

Practice

Complete the sentences with *for* or *since*.

1. Mark and Yolanda have been married _____*for*_____ 22 years.

2. They have been at the same address _____ 1992.

3. Yolanda has been a teacher _____ 1990.

4. Mark has been a salesman _____ 25 years.

5. He has been with the same company _____ 1995.

6. Now Mark is in Texas on a business trip. He has been there _____

   last Monday.

7. Mark has been on four business trips _____ last June.

8. It's Saturday. Yolanda is at the shopping center. She has been there _____

   10:00 this morning. She wants to get a birthday present for her son, Clark. He is

   16 today.

9. Yolanda has been busy _____ yesterday. She wants to prepare for Clark's

   birthday.

10. Right now Clark is at the school gym. He has been there _____ 9:00

    this morning.

11. Clark has been at the gym _____ three hours now.

12. He has been on the school basketball team _____ a year.

13. Clark has also been the top student in his class _____ three years.

14. Nick has been Clark's best friend _____ 1996.

15. Nick and Clark have been in the same class _____ many years.

16. Nick is always with Clark. Nick has been with Clark _____ this morning.

Your Turn

A.
Talk about yourself. Complete the following.

1. I came to this school in (month, year) _September, 20XX_ .

2. I have been here since _____.

3. I have been here for _____.

B.
Talk about your partner. Find out and then complete the following.

1. My friend's name is _____.

2. He/she came to this school in (month, year) _____.

3. He/she has been here since _____.

4. He/she has been here for _____.

5. We have been in this class since _____.

6. We have been in this class for _____.

C.
Tell the class about yourself and your partner.

Example:
I have been in this school since September.
My partner has been here for three months.

14b The Present Perfect Tense: Regular and Irregular Verbs

Form

1. We form the present perfect with *have/has* and the past participle of the verb.

2. We form the past participle of regular verbs by adding *-ed* to the verb. This is the same form as the simple past tense: *play, played*   *finish, finished*

3. Irregular verbs have irregular past participles: *know, known*   *write, written*

Regular Verbs	Simple Past	Past Participle
work	worked	**worked**
live	lived	**lived**
own	owned	**owned**
study	studied	**studied***

* Use the same spelling rules for the simple past and for the past participle.

Irregular Verbs	Simple Past	Past Participle
be	was/were	**been**
have	had	**had**
know	knew	**known**
go	went	**gone**
see	saw	**seen**

AFFIRMATIVE STATEMENTS				
Subject	*Have/Has*	Past Participle		*For/Since*
I	**have**	**had**		
You				
He/She/It	**has**	**owned**	a grammar book	**for** six months.
We	**have**	**studied**		**since** June.
They				

4 Practice

Complete the following sentences with the present perfect of the verb in parentheses.

Belton is a small town. Brad Peltry (live) _____*has lived*_____ in Belton all his life.
<u>1</u>

Brad is 58 years old. Brad is married. He (be) _____ married to Dora for 25
<u>2</u>

years. They (know) _____ each other since high school. Brad and Dora have
<u>3</u>

a son. He is a student at a university in Atlanta. He (study) _____ medicine
<u>4</u>

for three years now.

Brad owns the grocery store in town. He (own) _____the store for 22
<u>5</u>

years. He (work) _____ in the store for 22 years. Something strange has
<u>6</u>

happened this week. Nobody (see) _____ Brad for four days.
<u>7</u>

His truck (disappear) _____. Dora doesn't know where he is. Dora
<u>8</u>

(be) _____ worried. Brad (have) _____ money problems
<u>9</u>   <u>10</u>

lately.

5 What Do You Think?

What do you think has happened to Brad?

6 Read

A.
Read the following story. Then answer the questions.

Bob

Jim

The Poor Brother and the Rich Brother

Bob and Jim are brothers. They both grew up on a farm in Texas, in the United States. Bob is 75 and Jim is 73 now. When Bob was 16, he left school. He worked on his father's farm. When his father died, Bob took over the farm. Bob has lived on the farm all his life. When Bob was 20, he married Brenda. Brenda was another farmer's daughter. Bob and Brenda have been married for 55 years. They have been very happy. They have three children and twelve grandchildren. Bob says he has had a good life.

Jim didn't like life on the farm. When he was 16, he left the farm. He went to New York. Jim has had an interesting life. He has made a lot of money in business. At age 24 he was a very rich man. He has been married three times and divorced three times. His family life has been unhappy. He has two children, but his children don't love him. They haven't spoken to their father for many years. Jim has lived alone in his luxury villa in the south of France for ten years. Jim has visited many countries since he was 24 and he has made a lot of money, but is he happy? Jim thinks about his brother. He has not seen him since he was 16. But Bob has written to him every Christmas. He has sent him pictures of his family for 30 years. Jim has decided to visit his brother in Texas this Christmas.

B.
Write complete sentences about the story. Use the verbs from the list and the present perfect tense.

be – was/were – been	make – made – made	speak – spoke – spoken
have – had – had	see – saw – seen	visit – visited – visited
live – lived – lived	send – sent – sent	write – wrote – written

1. Bob/live/on the farm all his life

_Bob has lived on the farm all his life_____.

2. Bob and Brenda/be married/for 55 years

_____.

3. Bob and Brenda/be/happy

_____.

4. Bob/have/a good life

_____.

5. Jim/have/an interesting life

_____.

6. Jim's family life/be/unhappy

_____.

7. Jim/visit/many countries

_____.

8. Jim/make/a lot of money

_____.

9. Jim/live/alone for ten years

_____.

10. Bob/write to/Jim every Christmas

_____.

11. Bob/send/pictures of his family to Jim

_____.

12. Bob/not see/Jim for a long time

_____.

C.
Discuss and answer these questions with a partner.

1. What does Bob think about his life?

2. What does Jim think about his life?

3. Which brother has had a better life? Why?

14c The Present Perfect Tense: Negative Statements and Questions

Laura: **Have you lived** here long?

Sam: **No, I haven't.**

NEGATIVE STATEMENTS				
Subject	*Have/Has Not*	Past Participle		*For/Since*
I You We They	**have not** **haven't**	**lived** **been**	here	**for** a long time.
He She It	**has not** **hasn't**			

YES/NO QUESTIONS				SHORT ANSWERS	
Have/Has	Subject	Past Participle of Verb		Affirmative	Negative
Have	I			**Yes,**	**No,**
	you	**been** **lived**	here long?	you **have.**	you **haven't.**
	we			I/we **have.**	I/we **haven't.**
	they			you **have.**	you **haven't.**
Has	he			they **have.**	they **haven't.**
	she			he **has.**	he **hasn't.**
	it			she **has.**	she **hasn't.**
				it **has.**	it **hasn't.**

WH- QUESTIONS				
Wh- Word	*Have/Has*	Subject	Past Participle of Verb	
How long	**have**	I	**lived** **been**	here?
		you		
		we		
		they		
	has	he		
		she		
		it		

7 Practice

Complete the sentences using the present perfect tense of the verbs in parentheses.

A.

Alex: How long (be) __*have*__ you __*been*__ in this class?
　　　　　　　　　　　1　　　　　　　2

Peter: Since February.

Alex: (make) _____ you _____ any friends?
　　　　　　　　3　　　　　　　　　　4

Peter: Yes, I (make) _____ a lot of friends in this class, but my
　　　　　　　　　　　　　5

English (not, improve) _____.
　　　　　　　　　　　　　　　　6

B.

John: How long (have) _____ you _____ your driver's license?
                                 1   2

Bob: For two years.

John: (have) _____ you _____ any accidents?
                  3   4

Bob: No, I _____.
                  5

C.

Leyla: How long (study) _____ you _____ English?
                       1   2

Yumi: For six years, but I (not, speak) _____ English with
                                                   3
American people in a long time.

Leyla: Me neither. I (not, speak) _____ English with English or American
                                        4
people, but I (watch) _____ American movies for many years.
                           5

D.

Sue: How long (work) _____ you _____ here?
                  1   2

Don: Since May. But I (be) _____ a computer programmer for four years.
                         3

Sue: (work) _____ you _____ for other companies?
          4   5

Don: Yes, I _____. I (work) _____ for three companies
              6   7
since the year 2000.

Sue: (live) _____ you _____ in Boston since 2000?
         8   9

Don: Yes, I _____. I like Boston. How long (live) _____ you
           10   11
_____ in Boston?
   12

Sue: For three months now, and the weather (not, be) _____ good for the
                                         13
last three months. It (be) _____ so cold.
                        14

E.

Lillian: How long (be) _____ John _____ married?
                       1   2

Andrea: He (be) _____ married for six months, but he
                3
(know) _____ his wife for ten years.
          4

14d The Present Perfect Tense: *Ever* and *Never*

Ken: Have you **ever** been to Hawaii?
Brenda: No, I've **never** been to Hawaii.

1. We often use *ever* with the present perfect to ask questions. *Ever* means at any time up to now.

2. We use *never* to answer in the negative. *Never* means at no time up to now.

    Ken: Have you **ever** visited Australia?
    Brenda: No, I haven't.   OR   No, I've **never** visited Australia.

Have/Has	Subject	Ever/Never	Past Participle	
Have	you	**ever**	been	to Bangkok?

Subject	Have/Has	Ever/Never	Past Participle	
I	have	**never**	been	to Bangkok.

8 | Read

Do you remember Bob from Exercise 6? Read some more about Bob.

> Bob has lived on the farm all his life. Bob loves the simple farm life. He loves nature and animals. He is not interested in city life, expensive restaurants, or expensive clothes and cars. He spends his vacations camping and fishing near his home with his family. He has not gone outside his small town, and he doesn't want to. Bob doesn't want to be a millionaire. He just wants to stay on his farm and enjoy his family.

A.
Work with a partner. Make questions with the words. Your partner answers.

Example:
Bob/ever/be/to Europe
You: Has Bob ever been to Europe?
Your partner: No, he hasn't./No, he has never been to Europe.

1. Bob/ever/take/a plane
2. Bob/ever/visit/New York
3. Bob/ever/eat/sushi
4. Bob/ever/wear expensive clothes
5. Bob/ever/drink/champagne
6. Bob/ever/drive/expensive cars
7. Bob/ever/want/to be a millionaire
8. Bob/ever/go/to Paris
9. Bob/ever/work/in the city

B.
Write two more questions about Bob and answer them.

1. _____ ?
   _____ .
2. _____ ?
   _____ .

9 Practice

Work with a partner. Ask and answer questions with *ever* and *never*.

Example:
you/ever/be/to Australia
You: Have you ever been to Australia?
Your partner: Yes, I have.   OR   No, I haven't.

1. you/ever/meet/a famous person
2. you/ever/drive/a Ferrari
3. you/ever/swim/in the sea
4. you/ever/see/the Taj Mahal in India
5. you/ever/work/in a restaurant
6. you/ever/live/on a boat
7. you/ever/have/a motorcycle
8. you/ever/stay/in a five-star hotel
9. you/ever/read/Shakespeare

WRITING: Describe Experiences

Write a paragraph about your experiences in a class.

Step 1.   Think about your English class. Ask yourself the following questions.

1. How long have you studied English? (Two years, three years, six months?)
2. When did this English class start?
3. Who is your teacher?
4. How many students are in your class?
5. Have you made any friends in this class?
6. What grammar structures have you studied since the class started? (simple present, simple past, etc.)
7. What grammar structures have been the hardest?
8. How long did you study the simple past?
9. How long have you studied the present perfect?
10. How many tests have you had since the class started?
11. When was the last test?
12. How did you do on the test?

Step 2.   Write your answers in sentences.

Step 3.   Rewrite your sentences in paragraph form. Write a title in three to five words, for example, "My English Class". For more writing guidelines, see pages 190-195.

Step 4.   Evaluate your paragraph.

Checklist

_____   Did you use the verb tenses correctly?
_____   Did you answer all of the questions?
_____   Did you organize your answers into paragraphs?

Step 5.   Work with a partner to edit your sentences. Correct spelling, punctuation, vocabulary, and grammar.

Step 6.   Write your final copy.

SELF-TEST

A Choose the best answer, A, B, C, or D, to complete the sentence. Mark your answer by darkening the oval with the same letter.

1. _____ to Europe?

   A. Have you ever been   Ⓐ Ⓑ Ⓒ Ⓓ
   B. Ever been you
   C. Been ever
   D. Were you ever

2. Danny's not here. He _____ to the office an hour ago.

   A. went   Ⓐ Ⓑ Ⓒ Ⓓ
   B. was going
   C. has gone
   D. has went

3. We _____ to India.

   A. never have been   Ⓐ Ⓑ Ⓒ Ⓓ
   B. been never have
   C. have never been
   D. have been never

4. We _____ grammar since early this morning.

   A. studied   Ⓐ Ⓑ Ⓒ Ⓓ
   B. have to study
   C. have study
   D. have studied

5. A: Have you ever had a dog?
   B: Yes, I _____.

   A. have had   Ⓐ Ⓑ Ⓒ Ⓓ
   B. have
   C. had
   D. do

6. Nick _____ since yesterday.

   A. have not called   Ⓐ Ⓑ Ⓒ Ⓓ
   B. hasn't call
   C. did not call
   D. hasn't called

7. We _____ to a movie for a long time.

   A. haven't been   Ⓐ Ⓑ Ⓒ Ⓓ
   B. weren't
   C. haven't be
   D. haven't go

8. When _____?

   A. the movie starts   Ⓐ Ⓑ Ⓒ Ⓓ
   B. has the movie start
   C. did the movie start
   D. the movie has started

9. I _____ my mother yesterday.

   A. have called   Ⓐ Ⓑ Ⓒ Ⓓ
   B. was calling
   C. called
   D. have call

10. How long _____ ?

    A. have been married John   Ⓐ Ⓑ Ⓒ Ⓓ
    B. married John
    C. has John been married
    D. did marry John

B Find the underlined word or phrase, A, B, C, or D, that is incorrect. Mark your answer by darkening the oval with the same letter.

1. Humans lived on Earth for millions of
   A   B   C

   years.
   D

   Ⓐ Ⓑ Ⓒ Ⓓ

2. The weather has change in the last ten
   A   B   C

   years.
   D

   Ⓐ Ⓑ Ⓒ Ⓓ

3. There were many earthquakes in California
   A   B   C   D

   since 1914.

   Ⓐ Ⓑ Ⓒ Ⓓ

4. The president is not been in the country
   A   B

   since last Wednesday.
   C   D

   Ⓐ Ⓑ Ⓒ Ⓓ

5. Students had problems
   A   B

   with English spelling for a long time.
   C   D

   Ⓐ Ⓑ Ⓒ Ⓓ

6. This was the hottest summer since 1964.
   A   B   C   D

   Ⓐ Ⓑ Ⓒ Ⓓ

7. People have played soccer since four
   A   B

   hundred years.
   C   D

   Ⓐ Ⓑ Ⓒ Ⓓ

8. Mozart has written 600 pieces of music
   A   B   C

   before he died in 1891.
   D

   Ⓐ Ⓑ Ⓒ Ⓓ

9. Did you gone to Singapore when you lived
   A   B   C

   in Asia?
   D

   Ⓐ Ⓑ Ⓒ Ⓓ

10. Since 1990, scientists found many
    A   B

    new drugs to help us fight diseases.
    C   D

    Ⓐ Ⓑ Ⓒ Ⓓ

APPENDICES

Appendix 1   Grammar Terms

Adjective
An adjective describes a noun or a pronoun.

My cat is very **intelligent**.

He's **orange** and **white**.

Adverb
An adverb describes a verb, another adverb, or an adjective.

Joey speaks **slowly**.

Joey **always** visits his father on Wednesdays.

His father cooks **extremely** well.

His father is a **very** talented chef.

Article
An article comes before a noun. The definite article is *the*. The indefinite articles are *a* and *an*.

I read **an** online story and **a** magazine feature about celebrity lifestyles.

The online story was much more interesting than **the** magazine feature.

Auxiliary Verb
An auxiliary verb is found with a main verb. It is often called a "helping" verb.

Susan **can't** play in the game this weekend.

Does Ruth play baseball?

Where **does** Ruth play baseball?

Base Form
The base form of a verb has no tense. It has no endings (*–ed, –s,* or *–ing*).

Jill didn't **see** the band.

She should **see** them the next time they are in town.

Comparative
Comparative forms compare two things. They can compare people, places, or things.

This orange is **sweeter than** that grapefruit.

Working in a large city is **more stressful than** working in a small town.

Conjunction

A conjunction joins two or more sentences, adjectives, nouns, or prepositional phrases. Some conjunctions are *and, but,* and *or.*

> Kasey is efficient, **and** her work is excellent.
>
> Her apartment is small **but** comfortable.
>
> She works Wednesdays **and** Thursdays.

Contraction

A contraction is composed of two words put together with an apostrophe. Some letters are left out.

> Frank usually **doesn't** answer his phone.　　(doesn't = does + not)
>
> **He's** really busy.　　(he's = he + is)
>
> Does he know what time **we're** meeting?　　(we're = we + are)

Imperative

An imperative gives a command or directions. It uses the base form of the verb, and it does not use the word *you.*

> Please **tell** me how to get there.
>
> **Go** to the corner and **turn** left.

Modal

A modal is a type of auxiliary verb. The modal auxiliaries are *can, could, may, might, must, shall, should, will,* and *would.*

> Elizabeth **will** act the lead role in the play next week.
>
> She **couldn't** go to the party last night because she had to practice her lines.
>
> She **may** be able to go to the party this weekend.

Noun

A noun is a person, an animal, a place, or a thing.

> My **brother** and **sister-in-law** live in **Pennsylvania.**
>
> They have three **cats.**
>
> Their favorite sports are **skiing** and **cycling.**

Object

An object is the noun or pronoun that receives the action of the verb.

> Georgie sent **a gift** for Johnny's birthday.
>
> Johnny thanked **her** for the gift.

Preposition

A preposition is a small connecting word that is followed by a noun or pronoun. Some are a*t, above, after, by, before, below, for, in, of, off, on, over, to, under, up,* and *with*.

Every day, Jay drives Chris and Ally **to** school **in** the new car.

In the afternoon, he waits **for** them **at** the bus stop.

Pronoun

A pronoun takes the place of a noun.

Chris loves animals. **He** has two dogs and two cats.

His pets are very friendly. **They** like to spend time with people.

Sentence

A sentence is a group of words that has a subject and a verb. It is complete by itself.

Sentence: Brian works as a lawyer.

Not a sentence: Works as a lawyer.

Subject

A subject is the noun or pronoun that does the action in the sentence.

Trisha is from Canada.

She writes poetry about nature.

Superlative

Superlative forms compare three or more people, places, or things.

Jennifer is **the tallest** girl in the class.

She is from Paris, which is **the most romantic** city in the world.

Tense

Tense tells when the action in a sentence happens.

Simple present	–	The cat **eats** fish every morning.
Present progressive	–	He **is eating** fish now.
Simple past	–	He **ate** fish yesterday morning.
Past progressive	–	He **was eating** when the doorbell rang.
Future with *be going to*	–	He **is going to eat** fish tomorrow morning too!
Future with *will*	–	I think that he **will eat** the same thing next week.

Verb

A verb tells the action in a sentence.

Melissa **plays** guitar in a band.

She **loves** writing new songs.

The band **has** four other members.

Appendix 2   Numbers and Calendar Information

Numbers

Cardinal Numbers

1	=	one
2	=	two
3	=	three
4	=	four
5	=	five
6	=	six
7	=	seven
8	=	eight
9	=	nine
10	=	ten
11	=	eleven
12	=	twelve
13	=	thirteen
14	=	fourteen
15	=	fifteen
16	=	sixteen
17	=	seventeen
18	=	eighteen
19	=	nineteen
20	=	twenty
21	=	twenty-one
22	=	twenty-two
23	=	twenty-three
24	=	twenty-four
25	=	twenty-five
26	=	twenty-six
27	=	twenty-seven
28	=	twenty-eight
29	=	twenty-nine
30	=	thirty
40	=	forty
50	=	fifty

Ordinal Numbers

1st	=	first
2nd	=	second
3rd	=	third
4th	=	fourth
5th	=	fifth
6th	=	sixth
7th	=	seventh
8th	=	eighth
9th	=	ninth
10th	=	tenth
11th	=	eleventh
12th	=	twelfth
13th	=	thirteenth
14th	=	fourteenth
15th	=	fifteenth
16th	=	sixteenth
17th	=	seventeenth
18th	=	eighteenth
19th	=	nineteenth
20th	=	twentieth
21st	=	twenty-first
22nd	=	twenty-second
23rd	=	twenty-third
24th	=	twenty-fourth
25th	=	twenty-fifth
26th	=	twenty-sixth
27th	=	twenty-seventh
28th	=	twenty-eighth
29th	=	twenty-ninth
30th	=	thirtieth
40th	=	fortieth
50th	=	fiftieth

Cardinal Numbers

60	=	sixty
70	=	seventy
80	=	eighty
90	=	ninety
100	=	one hundred
200	=	two hundred
1,000	=	one thousand
10,000	=	ten thousand
100,000	=	one hundred thousand
1,000,000	=	one million

Ordinal Numbers

60th	=	sixtieth
70th	=	seventieth
80th	=	eightieth
90th	=	ninetieth
100th	=	one hundredth
200th	=	two hundredth
1,000th	=	one thousandth
10,000th	=	ten thousandth
100,000th	=	one hundred thousandth
1,000,000th	=	one millionth

Calendar Information

Days of the Week

	Abbreviation
Monday	Mon.
Tuesday	Tue.
Wednesday	Wed.
Thursday	Thurs.
Friday	Fri.
Saturday	Sat.
Sunday	Sun.

Months of the year

	Abbreviation
January	Jan.
February	Feb.
March	Mar.
April	Apr.
May	May
June	Jun.
July	Jul.
August	Aug.
September	Sept.
October	Oct.
November	Nov.
December	Dec.

Appendix 3   Irregular Verbs

Base Form	Simple Past	Past Participle	Base Form	Simple Past	Past Participle
be	was, were	been	keep	kept	kept
become	became	become	know	knew	known
begin	began	begun	leave	left	left
bend	bent	bent	lend	lent	lent
bite	bit	bitten	lose	lost	lost
blow	blew	blown	make	made	made
break	broke	broken	meet	met	met
bring	brought	brought	pay	paid	paid
build	built	built	put	put	put
buy	bought	bought	read	read	read
catch	caught	caught	ride	rode	ridden
choose	chose	chosen	ring	rang	rung
come	came	come	run	ran	run
cost	cost	cost	say	said	said
cut	cut	cut	see	saw	seen
do	did	done	sell	sold	sold
draw	drew	drawn	send	sent	sent
drink	drank	drunk	shake	shook	shaken
drive	drove	driven	shut	shut	shut
eat	ate	eaten	sing	sang	sung
fall	fell	fallen	sit	sat	sat
feed	fed	fed	sleep	slept	slept
feel	felt	felt	speak	spoke	spoken
fight	fought	fought	spend	spent	spent
find	found	found	stand	stood	stood
fly	flew	flown	steal	stole	stolen
forget	forgot	forgotten	swim	swam	swum
get	got	gotten/got	take	took	taken
give	gave	given	teach	taught	taught
go	went	gone	tear	tore	torn
grow	grew	grown	tell	told	told
hang	hung	hung	think	thought	thought
have	had	had	throw	threw	thrown
hear	heard	heard	understand	understood	understood
hide	hid	hidden	wake up	woke up	woken up
hit	hit	hit	wear	wore	worn
hold	held	held	win	won	won
hurt	hurt	hurt	write	wrote	written

Appendix 4 Spelling Rules for Endings

Adding a Final –s to Nouns and Verbs

Rule	Example	-s
1. For most words, add –s without making any changes.	book bet save play	books bets saves plays
2. For words ending in a consonant + *y*, change the *y* to *i* and add –es.	study party	studies parties
3. For words ending in *ch, s, sh, x,* or *z*, add –es.	church class wash fix quiz	churches classes washes fixes quizzes
4. For words ending in *o*, sometimes add –es and sometimes add –s.	potato piano	potatoes pianos
5. For words ending in *f* or *lf*, change the *f* or *lf* to *v* and add –es. For words ending in *fe*, change the *f* to *v* and add –s.	loaf half life	loaves halves lives

Adding a Final *-ed*, *-er*, *-est*, and *-ing*

Rule	Example	*-ed*	*-er*	*-est*	*-ing*
1. For most words, add the ending without making any changes.	clean	cleaned	cleaner	cleanest	cleaning
2. For words ending in silent *e*, drop the *e* and add the ending.	save like nice	saved liked	saver nicer	 nicest	saving liking
3. For words ending in a consonant + *y*, change the *y* to *i* and add *-ed*, *-er*, or *-est*. Do not change or drop the *y* before adding *-ing*.	sunny happy study worry	 studied worried	sunnier happier	sunniest happiest	 studying worrying
4. For one-syllable words ending in one vowel and one consonant, double the final consonant, then add the ending. Do not double the last consonant if it is a *w, x,* or *y*.	hot run bat glow mix stay	 batted glowed mixed stayed	hotter runner batter mixer	hottest	 running batting glowing mixing staying
5. For words of two or more syllables that end in one vowel and one consonant, double the final consonant if the final syllable is stressed.	begin refer occur permit	 referred occurred permitted	beginner		beginning referring occurring permitting
6. For words of two or more syllables that end in one vowel and one consonant, do NOT double the final consonant if the final syllable is NOT stressed.	enter happen develop	entered happened developed	 developer		entering happening developing

Appendix 5   Capitalization Rules

First words

1. Capitalize the first word of every sentence.

   They live in San Francisco.   **W**hat is her name?

2. Capitalize the first word of a quotation.

   She said, "**M**y name is Nancy."

Names

1. Capitalize names of people, including titles of address.

   Mr. Thompson   **A**lison **E**mmet   **M**ike **A. L**ee

2. Capitalize the word "I".

   Rose and **I** went to the market.

3. Capitalize nationalities, ethnic groups, and religions.

   Korean   **L**atino   **A**sian   **I**slam

4. Capitalize family words if they appear alone or with a name, but not if they have a possessive pronoun or article.

   Where's **D**ad?   vs.   Where's my **f**ather?

   He's at **A**unt Lucy's house.   vs.   He's at an **a**unt's house.

Places

1. Capitalize the names of countries, states, cities, and geographical areas.

   Mexico   **V**irginia   **T**okyo   the **S**outh

2. Capitalize the names of oceans, lakes, rivers, and mountains.

   the **P**acific **O**cean   **L**ake **O**ntario   the **N**ile   **M**t. **E**verest

3. Capitalize the names of streets, schools, parks, and buildings.

   Main **S**treet   **C**entral **P**ark

   the **U**niversity of **C**alifornia   the **E**mpire **S**tate **B**uilding

4. Don't capitalize directions if they aren't names of geographical areas.

   She lives **n**ortheast of Washington.   We fly **s**outh during our flight.

Time words

1. Capitalize the names of days and months.

   Monday   Friday   January   September

2. Capitalize the names of holidays and historical events.

   Christmas   Independence Day   World War I

3. Don't capitalize the names of seasons.

   spring   summer   fall   winter

Titles

1. Capitalize the first word and all important words of titles of books, magazines, newspapers, and articles.

   The Sound and the Fury   *Time Out*

   The New York Times   "The Influence of Hip Hop"

2. Capitalize the first word and all important words of titles of films, plays, radio programs, and TV shows.

   Star Wars   *A Midsummer Night's Dream*

   "All Things Considered"   "Friends"

3. Don't capitalize articles (*a, an, the*), conjunctions (*but, and, or*) and short prepositions (*of, with, in, on, for*) unless they are the first word of a title.

   The Story of Cats   *The Woman in the Dunes*

Appendix 6   Punctuation Rules

Period

1. Use a period at the end of a statement or command.

   I live in New York.   Open the door.

2. Use a period after most abbreviations.

   Ms.   Dr.   St.   U.S.

   Exceptions: NATO   UN   AIDS   IBM

3. Use a period after initials.

   Ms. K.L. Kim   F.C. Simmons

Question Mark

1. Use a question mark at the end of questions.

   Is he working tonight?   Where did they used to work?

2. In a direct quotation, the question mark goes before the quotation marks.

   Martha asked, "What's the name of the street?"

Exclamation Point

Use an exclamation point at the end of exclamatory sentences or phrases. They express surprise or extreme emotion.

   Wow!   I got an A!

Comma

1. Use a comma to separate items in a series.

   John will have juice, coffee, and tea at the party.

2. Use a comma to separate two or more adjectives that each modify the noun alone.

   Purrmaster is a smart, friendly cat. (*smart* and *friendly* cat)

3. Use a comma before a conjunction (*and, but, or, so*) that separates two independent clauses.

   The book is very funny, and the film is funny too.

   She was tired, but she didn't want to go to sleep.

4. Don't use a comma before a conjunction that separates two phrases that aren't complete sentences.

   I worked in a bakery at night and went to class during the day.

   Do you want to see a band or go to a club?

5. Use a comma after an introductory clause or phrase.

> After we hike the first part of the trail, we are going to rest.
>
> If you exercise every day, you will be healthy.

6. Use a comma after *yes* and *no* in answers.

> Yes, that is my book.
>
> No, I'm not.

7. Use a comma to separate nonrestrictive clauses from the rest of a sentence. A nonrestrictive clause gives more information about the noun it describes, but it isn't needed to identify the noun.

> Kevin's new computer, which he needs for work, has a lot of memory.
>
> *Esperanto*, which has Flamenco dancing on Wednesdays, is our favorite restaurant.

8. Use a comma to separate quotations from the rest of a sentence. Don't use a comma if the quotation is a question and it is in the first part of the sentence.

> The student said, "I'm finished with the homework."
>
> "I'm also finished," added his friend.
>
> "Are you really finished?" asked the student.

Apostrophe

1. Use apostrophes in contractions.

> don't (*do not*)   it's (*it is*)   he's (*he is*)   we're (*we are*)

2. Use apostrophes to show possession.

> Anne's book (the book belongs to Anne)

Quotation marks

1. Use quotation marks at the beginning and end of exact quotations. Other punctuation marks go before the end quotation marks.

> Burt asked, "When are we leaving?"
>
> "Right after lunch," Mark replied.

2. Use quotation marks before and after titles of articles, songs, stories, and television shows. Most commonly, periods and commas are placed before the end quotation marks, while question marks and exclamation points are placed after them. If the title is a question, the question mark is placed inside the quotation marks and appropriate punctuation is placed at the end of the sentence.

> Burt's favorite song is "Show Some Emotion" by Joan Armatrading.
>
> He read an article called "Motivating Your Employees."
>
> We read an interesting article called "How Do You Motivate Employees?".

Italics and Underlining

1. If you are writing on a computer, use italic type (*like this*) for books, newspapers, magazines, films, plays, and words from other languages.

   Have you ever read *Woman in the Dunes*?

   The only magazine she reads is *The Economist*.

   How do you say *buenos dias* in Chinese?

2. If you are writing by hand, underline the titles of books, newspapers, magazines, films, and plays.

   Have you ever read <u>Woman in the Dunes</u>?

   The only magazine she reads is <u>The Economist</u>.

   How do you say <u>buenos dias</u> in Chinese?

Appendix 7   Writing Basics

1. Sentence types

There are three types of sentences: declarative, interrogative, and exclamatory. Declarative sentences state facts and describe events, people, or things. We use a period at the end of these sentences. Interrogative sentences ask yes/no questions and wh- questions. We use a question mark at the end of these sentences. Exclamatory sentences express surprise or extreme emotion, such as joy or fear. We use an exclamation point at the end of these sentences.

2. Indenting

We indent the first line of a paragraph. Each paragraph expresses a new thought, and indenting helps to mark the beginning of this new thought.

3. Writing titles

The title should give the main idea of a piece of writing. It should be interesting. It goes at the top of the composition and is not usually a complete sentence. In a title, capitalize the first word and all of the important words. Do not capitalize conjunctions (*and, but, so, or*), articles (*a, an, the*), or short prepositions (*at, by, for, in, of, on, out, to, up, with*) unless they are the first word of the title.

4. Writing topic sentences

The topic sentence tells the reader the main idea of the paragraph. It is always a complete sentence with a subject and a verb. It is often the first sentence in a paragraph, but sometimes it is in another position in the paragraph.

5. Organizing ideas

Information can be organized in a paragraph in different ways. One common way is to begin with a general idea and work toward more specific information. Another way is to give the information in order of time using words like *before, after, as, when, while,* and *then*.

6. Connecting ideas

It is important to connect the ideas in a paragraph so that the paragraph has cohesion. Connectors and transitional words help make the writing clear, natural, and easy to read. Connectors and transitional words include *and, in addition, also, so, but, however, for example, such as, so ... that,* and *besides*.

7. The writing process

Success in writing generally follows these basic steps:

❖ Brainstorm ideas.
❖ Organize the ideas.
❖ Write a first draft of the piece.
❖ Evaluate and edit the piece for content and form.
❖ Rewrite the piece.

Appendix 8 Maps

United States

Canada

SCALE

0   1000 Miles

0   1000 KM

Asia

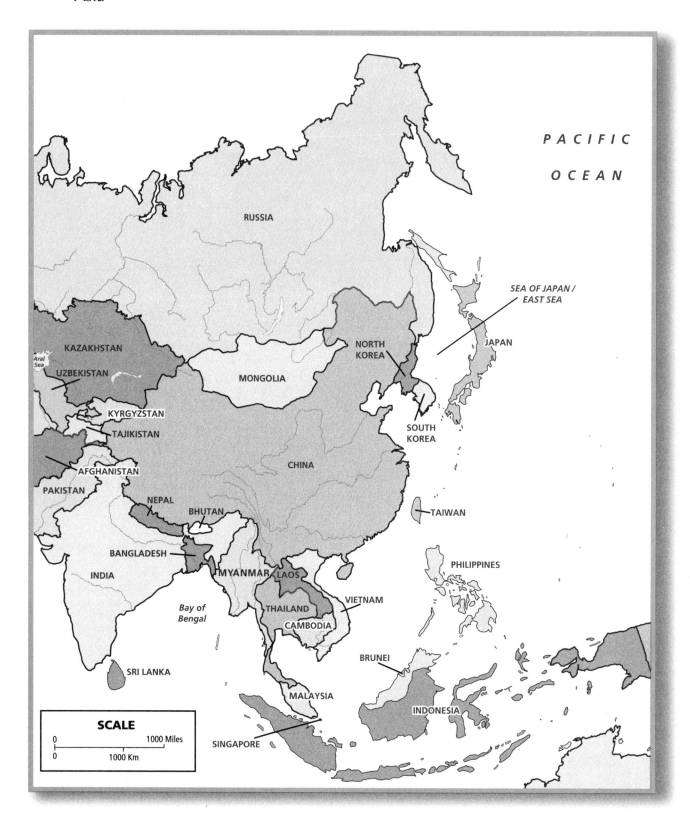

Appendices

Central and South America

Europe

Index